The Human Touch

D1523154

From left to right: Joan Mahanna (John G. W. Mahanna's daughter), President John F. Kennedy, and Jackie Kennedy.

The Human Touch

My Friendship and Work with President John F. Kennedy

John G. W. Mahanna

The Human Touch:

My Friendship and Work with President John F. Kennedy

Maurice Bassett
P.O. Box 839
Anna Maria, FL 34216

Contact the publisher:
MauriceBassett@gmail.com

Editing, research, and inside pages layout by Michael Pastore
Cover design and graphics by David Michael Moore

ISBN: 978-1-60025-173-3

Library of Congress Control Number: 2021941881

Contents

Introduction to *The Human Touch*

It is with great pleasure that I introduce my father's political relationship with President John F. Kennedy, written from a manuscript that I found many years ago packed away at my mother's home in Florida.

The manuscript was a compilation of typewritten pages as well as written notes, newspaper articles, and letters between my father and JFK. My father started his newspaper career in 1933 as a correspondent for his home town newspaper *The Berkshire Eagle*. He served on the county and city staffs of *The Berkshire Eagle* prior to being appointed County Editor in 1947. There was a break in his newspaper service from 1942–1945 when he was a Special Agent with the Office of Naval Intelligence and spent more than two years in combat duty with the amphibious forces of the Pacific Fleet.

During my father's Navy career he met John F. Kennedy, then a fellow Naval Officer in the Pacific. After Kennedy became a Congressman in Massachusetts with ambitions for statewide office, my father arranged a series of appearances for him in Berkshire County in 1946. When Kennedy decided to run for the U.S. Senate in 1952, additional appearances were outlined by my father throughout Massachusetts.

After Kennedy was elected President of the United States in 1960, Kennedy appointed my father Public Information Officer with the Office of Civil Defense at the Pentagon. In 1971, my father was detailed to the Office of Emergency Preparations and then in 1973 to the Cost of Living Council as a Public-Affairs Specialist. When he retired in 1976, he held the title of National Organization Officer with the Defense Preparedness Agency.

My father was also author of two books. *Music Under the Moon* is an early history of the Berkshire Symphonic Festival at Tanglewood, located in Lenox, Massachusetts. *The Seated Lincoln* is a story about the creation of the Lincoln Memorial and statue of Abraham Lincoln.

Please enjoy this wonderful book.

Jonathan Mahanna
(Son of John G. W. Mahanna)

Dedicated to the memory of my father

John G. W. Mahanna

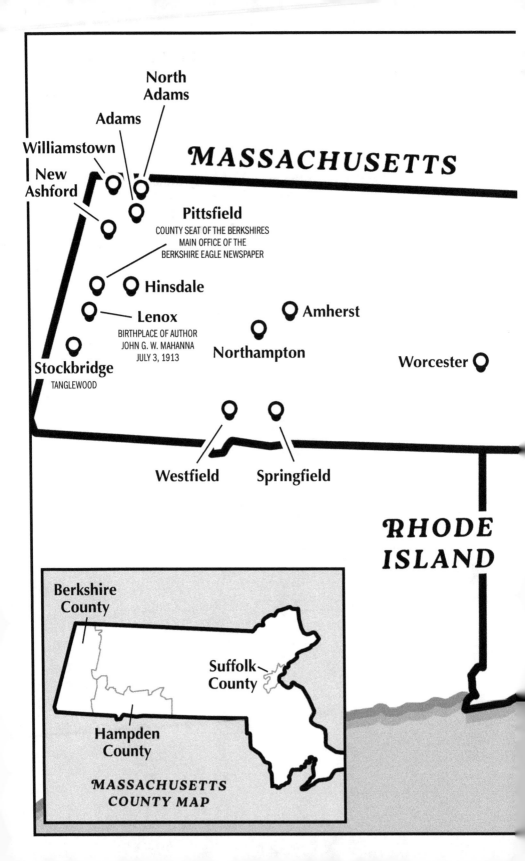

North
Adams

Adams

Williamstown

New
Ashford

MASSACHUSETTS

Pittsfield
COUNTY SEAT OF THE BERKSHIRES
MAIN OFFICE OF THE
BERKSHIRE EAGLE NEWSPAPER

Hinsdale

Amherst

Lenox
BIRTHPLACE OF AUTHOR
JOHN G. W. MAHANNA
JULY 3, 1913

Northampton

Worcester

Stockbridge
TANGLEWOOD

Westfield   Springfield

RHODE
ISLAND

Berkshire
County

Suffolk
County

Hampden
County

MASSACHUSETTS
COUNTY MAP

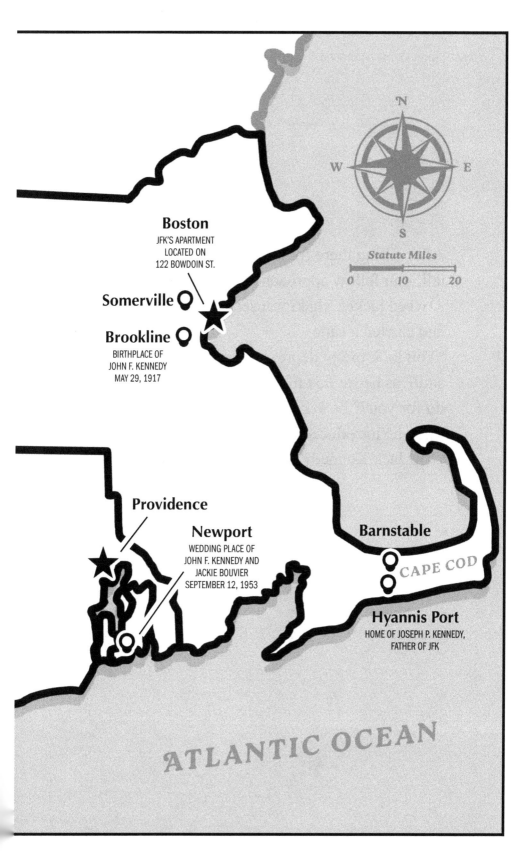

After sitting there for a few minutes, a handsome, tall, thin fellow approached me. He was dressed in a tweed jacket, khaki trousers, wore brown loafers and carried a cane.

"You look pretty depressed, pal," he said with a smile as he sat down beside me. "Anything I can do for you?" he asked.

Then he introduced himself.

"I'm Jack Kennedy. What is your name?"

1

April 1945
A Fortunate Meeting

W henever I see people sitting around a hotel lobby, I sometimes wonder if fate will take them through a path as exciting and depressing as the one I followed for more than 25 years — after first meeting the young man who became the 35th President of the United States, John Fitzgerald Kennedy.

Our meeting came quite by accident.

Upon returning to the West Coast from amphibious duty with the U.S. Navy in the South Pacific during World War II, I was hospitalized for a short time for an arthritic condition in my back and legs at the U.S. Naval Hospital in Treasure Island, outside of San Francisco.

Following examinations and treatments, I was given temporary duty orders with the Office of Naval Intelligence in the 12th Naval District Headquarters in San Francisco. I lost little time in heading for the Cliff Hotel where my orders specified a room had been reserved for me at the bachelor officers' quarters in the hotel.

The lobby of the hotel that dreary day in April 1945 was filled with people, many of whom I observed came from foreign countries. It was then I realized the United Nations Conference on International Organization was underway in the city.

After standing in line at the registration desk for nearly a half hour, I was stunned to learn from the room clerk there were no quarters available for U.S. Navy officers. They were all taken by foreign delegates, I was informed.

I appealed to the hotel manager, displayed my orders and explained I had just been discharged from the hospital after returning from the South Pacific. My rank, a chief warrant boatswain, didn't seem to impress him and he was of little assistance in helping me to solve my problem. After a brief visit, he suggested that I sit around the lobby for a while, hoping for a cancellation which he doubted would occur. Or, he felt, I should go downtown where my chances of getting a room in another hotel might be brighter.

My situation was bleak but not desperate. I knew my former ship, the U.S.S. Heywood (APA−6) was in dry dock for repairs at the navy yard and certainly my former shipmates could arrange for me to spend the night aboard giving me time the next day to find a place to stay. I felt too that if the Chief of Police of San Francisco, Charles Dellea, knew of my plight he might possibly use his influence to get me a room. His son, Eddie, was a classmate at the U.S. Navy Indoctrination School at the University of Arizona before I was shipped out to the South Pacific.

I chose to go downtown. Lugging a valpack containing my uniforms and another piece of luggage with more clothes, I hailed a cab and asked him to take me to one of the best hotels.

Within a short time he delivered me to the Palace Hotel where, he thought, my chances of getting a room would be better than at the Mark Hopkins, St. Francis, or Fairmount, all close by.

Upon entering the hotel lobby I soon learned it was the headquarters for the news media covering the Conference.

Being a former newspaperman in Massachusetts, this gave me some encouragement.

With baggage in hand, I nervously approached the registration desk with my simple request — a single room with bath.

The courteous clerk asked whether I had a reservation to which I naturally replied in the negative with a feeling of great depression. He listened to my review of the events of the day and appeared to be most sympathetic. Excusing himself for a moment, he entered a room in back of the desk where I noticed he was checking a long list of names, obviously the reservation list, looking for a cancellation. He returned with another clerk, who was about to relieve him, chatting quietly about my problem. Both agreed I should check my luggage and go back later to see either of them about cancellations. From the expressions on their faces I sensed the situation wasn't entirely hopeless. In fact, I was slightly encouraged for the first time that day.

As I wandered about the lobby, I kept thinking of Chief Dellea. Why not give him a call?

When I did, the desk sergeant could only advise me that the Chief was on a weekend Catholic retreat with a group of policemen from the department.

Disheartened, I kept walking through the lobby until I

noticed at the far end a sign, "Happy Valley Bar — Men Only."

That's for me, I thought, and walked through the swinging doors where I found the bar sparsely filled with civilians. Not a military man was in sight. It was 3 in the afternoon.

Before I seated myself on a stool, an amiable bartender extended his hand, introducing himself as "Tony."

"Beer?" he asked.

"No, thanks," I answered. "I feel like a Scotch and soda right now."

"Sorry," said Tony. "Guess you must be new in the area. The West Coast Military Command has a rigid rule that only beer can be served to military personnel in uniform until after 4 p.m."

I settled for a beer as Tony introduced me to a few of his regular customers.

Their eyes focused on the ribbons I wore on my uniform: the Presidential Unit Citation, six battle stars on the Pacific bar, and the Philippine Liberation award. Our conversation touched on my experiences in the South Pacific which I described briefly, leading up to the events of day which brought me into the Happy Valley Bar.

Soon the exchange of information with my newfound friends shifted to occupations. Tony's customers for the most part were employees of the Bank of America. The others were executives from nearby office buildings. When they learned I was a newspaper reporter in Massachusetts before the war, they became interested in whether any of the newspaper people covering the Conference were friends or acquaintances.

When I explained I didn't know who was in the city from

the New England papers since I had not read a Massachusetts paper in weeks, one of the group volunteered to pick up from the press headquarters off of the lobby a list of visiting reporters, columnists, and special writers. When he returned I studied the long list of names recognizing only two from Boston — Bill Cunningham of *The Herald* and Robert L. Norton of *The Post*.

While I was a reporter before the war working for *The Berkshire Eagle* in Pittsfield, Massachusetts, I was also a stringer in Berkshire County for *The Boston Post*, *The New York Times*, and *The New York Herald-Tribune*.

Periodically when I visited Boston, I would drop in to the editorial room of *The Post* to see Eddie Dunn, the city editor, who hired me as a stringer. On one of those occasions I met Bill Cunningham, who at the time was covering sports for *The Post*, transferring later to *The Herald*.

Robert L. Norton was not one of my acquaintances, but I was familiar with his byline which appeared in those days on page one of *The Post* with a Washington dateline over the heading: "Robert L. Norton comments ... "

I took leave of my friends, thanking them for their friendliness, and went into the lobby to check on cancellations at the registration desk.

"Nothing yet," reported the clerk, adding, "but don't go too far away. Something may break soon."

I mingled among the scores of people in the lobby hoping to see Bill Cunningham, a large, broad-shouldered man, whose athletic accomplishments during his college days at Dartmouth were well known to all New Englanders.

When I couldn't locate him, I went to a house phone and called his room but there was no answer.

Dejected, my thoughts turned to getting a taxi to take me to my former ship, the Heywood, in dry dock where I was sure to have a place to sleep for that night.

An empty couch in the lobby looked inviting so I decided to sit for a while and ponder my thoughts.

After sitting there for a few minutes, a handsome, tall, thin fellow approached me. He was dressed in a tweed jacket, khaki trousers, wore brown loafers and carried a cane.

"You look pretty depressed, pal," he said with a smile as he sat down beside me. "Anything I can do for you?" he asked.

Then he introduced himself.

"I'm Jack Kennedy. What is your name?"

When I answered, informing him of my Massachusetts background, he sparkled, wanting to be filled in on why I was in uniform sitting there alone in the lobby of the Palace Hotel.

Again I recited my day's activities — the return a few days ago from the South Pacific, the discharge from the Naval Hospital at Treasure Island, receiving new orders to ONI [Office of Naval Intelligence], being rebuffed at the Cliff House B.O.Q., and the desperate try I was making to find a room in a city where all hotels seemed to be occupied to capacity because of the San Francisco Conference.

In near disbelief, I had difficulty for a few minutes realizing that this meeting actually had happened. Slowly regaining my composure, there flashed through my mind, the suffering and heroism of this man on August 2, 1943 when his PT-109 Motor Torpedo Boat was cut in half and exploded after being hit amidships in the waters of Blackett Strait, west of New Georgia, by the Japanese destroyer, Amagiri.

He did not speak of his ordeal, but rather persisted in learning more about my hospitalization and the general condition of my health.

I felt embarrassed as he spoke, assuring him my arthritic problem was minor compared to the suffering he was experiencing.

Sitting there visiting with a war hero, given up for dead, whose yellowish complexion bore evidence of the malaria he had contracted in the South Pacific, was an unforgettable experience. The PT boat explosion had aggravated an old back injury and it was obvious to me that he was in great pain, occasionally shifting his weight around while seated on the couch. I had read many accounts of this brave young man's leadership in effecting the rescue of the surviving members of his crew on PT-109; the tragic death in 1944 of his brother, Joseph P. Kennedy Jr., who was killed when his bomber blew up on a mission for which he volunteered, aimed at destroying enemy submarine pens on the Belgian Coast.

At the same time I had recollections of other members of his family back in Massachusetts.

Two of his sisters attended a summer camp in the 1930s in Hinsdale, a small town east of Pittsfield, Massachusetts, where I lived and worked before joining the U.S. Navy. The camp, Fernside, was operated for many years by the Sullivan family of Lowell on the shores of Plunkett Lake in Hinsdale, 150 miles from Boston.

His father, Joseph P. Kennedy, had filled speaking

engagements in Berkshire County before he was appointed by President Franklin D. Roosevelt in 1937 as Ambassador to the Court of St. James. His grandfather, John F. (Honey) Fitzgerald had many followers among Irish Catholics in Berkshire County, resulting from his statewide campaigns for governor and more notably for the United States Senate in 1916, where he lost to the incumbent, Henry Cabot Lodge.

Jack rested his cane against an arm on the couch and sat down beside me. "What brings you here?" he asked.

After explaining I recently returned from the South Pacific where my ship participated in assault landings on atolls and islands with the amphibious forces of the Navy, was hospitalized for a few days at Treasure Island Naval Hospital and discharged only that morning with orders to report to the Office of Naval Intelligence and couldn't find a room, he smiled, put his hand on my shoulder, assuring me he "would work something out and don't worry."

As he inquired into my past, he lifted himself from the couch when I mentioned that, before the war, I was a reporter for *The Berkshire Eagle* in Pittsfield, Massachusetts. With that he picked up his cane, asking me to remain right there.

"I'll be back in a few minutes," he said as I saw him walk toward the hotel manager's office.

Back he came, accompanied by a nattily dressed executive, whom he introduced as the manager of the Palace Hotel.

"Meet John Mahanna, an old pal of mine," said Jack as the manager and I shook hands.

I tried not to show my embarrassment upon hearing Jack refer to me as "an old pal," but it sure gave me a lift in spirits.

"John needs a room and I hope you can help him," Jack told the manager, adding "if you can't find him a room tonight put a cot in my room and make him comfortable until you find one."

It sounded like an order as Jack winked at me.

"I'll do my best, Mr. Kennedy," the manager replied as he walked away and instructed me to check at the registration desk later in the evening.

"We'll make out, you can bet on it," Jack asserted as we continued our conversation on the hotel lobby couch. As we discussed our families, a wide grin spread across his face when he learned my mother's maiden name was Fitzgerald and that I had married a Kennedy girl, Evona, whose father was an eye, ear, nose, and throat specialist in Pittsfield.

"How can you miss, John, being the son of a Fitzgerald and married to a Kennedy!"

He seemed eager to learn more about my background. We covered the early 1930s when I became a town news correspondent and later a city staff reporter on *The Eagle*.

He was intrigued with my activities as a political reporter, an interest I told him developed as a teenager when Franklin D. Roosevelt visited my hometown, Lenox, in the 1928 Presidential campaign to stump for Al Smith, the Democratic candidate for President.

I described my recollection of that visit when FDR stepped from his limousine wearing braces and with the aid of canes mounted the steps of the wide veranda of the town's only hotel, the Curtis, a popular resort for many years. I related my experiences through the early years of serving *The Eagle* as a political reporter. He was especially interested in hearing about the rise of a dynamic lawyer from Springfield, Massachusetts, Thomas F. Moriarty who was one of the speakers at the Al Smith rally when FDR appeared in town. Moriarty, a former Georgetown University football player, went on to become elected district attorney of Western Massachusetts, a power in Massachusetts politics, and a strong supporter of Paul A. Dever, former attorney general and governor of Massachusetts.

Jack enjoyed hearing stories about James Michael Curley in the western part of the state during his campaigns for governor and U.S. Senator which I covered.

Jack knew them all, not intimately at the time perhaps, but he had an encyclopedic mind about leading politicians in both parties, especially in the Boston area.

He pressed me about the type of campaigns that were waged in the far western part of the state, obviously aware that the State House politicians seldom visited that part of the Commonwealth until just before election time. It never occurred to me then that he was probably forming a picture in his own mind on procedures to take at some later date. In fact, he volunteered that he was most interested in a career as a newspaperman or an author.

"It must be a fascinating life," he said.

"I like to write, too. That is why I am here writing my observations of the Conference for the Hearst wire service." With that he looked at his watch and realized he was late for an appointment with some foreign dignitary.

"How about having lunch with me here tomorrow about 12:30?" he asked.

"I would be happy to, Jack," I replied, not knowing when I checked into ONI headquarters in the morning whether my schedule would permit it, but I decided to take a chance.

As he was about to leave, he signaled me to accompany him to the hotel desk where he instructed the clerk to give me a key to his room and freshen up, explaining I had a standby reservation. With his key in my pocket, I started for the elevator when the hotel manager approached to let me know he had found a room for me on the seventh floor. When I handed him Jack's room key, my newfound friend smiled as he walked away, looking back over his shoulder saying, "See you at lunch. Leave a message in my box so I will know what room you are in."

2

April 1945
Adventures with the Journalists

Jack hadn't walked fifteen steps when he called to me as I was about to get on the elevator.

He had been intercepted by a journalist and wanted me to meet him. It was Bob Norton of *The Boston Post*. Bob was no fashion model. He wore a wrinkled suit, oversized topcoat and a soft hat which indicated it had traveled thousands of miles. His eyeglasses kept slipping down his nose and he talked so fast it was difficult to catch his every word.

When Jack told Bob I was a former reporter on *The Berkshire Eagle* and served as a stringer for *The Post* in Western Massachusetts he was delighted, taking from his pocket an invitation to a cocktail party and reception for the Massachusetts people identified with the Conference or living in the San Francisco area.

"The Swigs from Boston are throwing two parties, one at the Fairmount and the other at the St. Francis," Bob related enthusiastically. "They own both places."

"Are you going?" he asked Jack.

"No, I have another engagement, but why don't you take

John along?" Jack suggested.

"Fine," said Bob, "I'll meet you at the hotel desk in two hours." Then we went our separate ways.

I gathered my luggage from the porter, went to my room, unpacked, showered and shaved, put on my uniform and wrote a letter to my wife telling her in detail all that had happened that day.

I met Bob at the appointed hour and place. We took a cab to the Fairmount. As we entered the elevator to go to the fifth floor dining room, Bob recognized on the way up an old "friend," General Jan Christian Smuts, prime minister of the Union of South Africa, impeccably garbed in his military uniform. They had met before in Washington, during one of the general's conferences at the White House with President Franklin D. Roosevelt.

General Smuts, dignified and courteous, was doing his best to agree with Bob that they certainly had met once or twice before in Washington, as Bob, giving the prime minister a friendly tap on the back, described him as "a real guy." I cringed at this demonstration of affection — and security men escorting the general didn't appear to be overly pleased with the greeting, either.

As the elevator reached his floor, General Smuts and his entourage lost little time getting out, away from Bob, and then hastily walked to his suite.

When we entered the dining room, filled with Massachusetts people sipping cocktails and consuming cocktails, Bill Cunningham was entertaining a group at the piano. The sight of Cunningham, a former colleague on *The Post*, was too much for Bob.

Reaching for a highball from the nearest tray, Bob quickly drank it and started hurling a few unmentionable remarks in the direction of the former *Post* columnist. Bill's booming voice delivered his replies to Bob in such a way that anyone within hearing distance could sense they were not on very friendly terms.

Soon Bob recognized a few other acquaintances who engaged him in friendly conversation. What a relief. I was picturing myself as an innocent bystander in a personality clash between two well-known newspapermen, unaware that bad blood existed between them. Bob's friends coaxed him to try a few hors d'oeuvres which seemed to sustain him until we adjourned to the St. Francis Hotel for the buffet which helped to bring Bob back on a steady course.

Bob had mentioned he had to file a story that night for *The Post* but he wanted to think for a while about the subject. We returned to the Palace and from all outward appearances Bob made a good recovery from his twilight party tour. He insisted on taking a nap before starting to write his column. He asked me to call him in his room in an hour. Before falling on the covers of his bed he instructed me to "alert Charlie Brown that my copy will be ready for Western Union in about two hours."

Brown, who was well known to the press media from Presidential campaigns during the Roosevelt years, had been detailed by Western Union to San Francisco to handle wire stories from the Conference. I gave Charlie the message from Bob. After an hour had passed I dutifully telephoned Bob to inform him it was time to start writing.

At the other end of the line I heard an assortment of noises as Bob apparently dropped the phone after picking it up from its cradle. I could hear glass breaking and shouts of anger in the background.

Bob finally answered.

"John, for God's sake get up here fast. I was so startled when the phone rang that I fell out of bed reaching for it and my specs are broken. I can't see."

I rushed to his room, found the door unlocked. There was Bob on his hands and knees trying to pick up an overturned lamp, holding in his hand the frame of his eyeglasses with one lens missing and the other cracked. Scattered nearby were pieces of glass from a broken ice pitcher.

"You'll have to help me by typing the column," said Bob as he pulled himself into a chair next to his typewriter.

"Have you decided on a subject?" I inquired.

"Yes," he replied, "Jack Kennedy is going to be elected the next mayor of Boston."

I gulped as I sat in front of his typewriter, arranging carbons and ready to take his dictation.

This is strange, I thought, because Jack Kennedy did not indicate to me any desire to enter politics in Boston when I talked with him earlier. He seemed interested only in a writing career. He hadn't touched on politics in my short conversation with him in the hotel lobby, except to observe that delegates to the Conference were political leaders in their own countries, the policy makers of the world and architects of the future.

However, I was eager to learn what Bob Norton had in mind. Then he started dictating:

"James Michael Curley is in for the shock of his life," Bob exclaimed as I typed out the first sentence.

Continuing, he related:

"The next mayor of Boston will be John Fitzgerald Kennedy, that courageous young war hero in the South Pacific, the son of the former U.S. Ambassador to the Court of St. James, Joseph P. Kennedy, and the grandson of the beloved former mayor of Boston, John F. (Honey) Fitzgerald."

With tongue in cheek, I hung on to every word as Bob continued to dictate his masterpiece. In a blistering attack on Curley, he covered the Purple Shamrock's unsuccessful attempt to become a U.S. Senator, his defeat at the polls by young Maurice J. Tobin as mayor of Boston, and his loss to Leverett Saltonstall in his bid for election as governor of the Commonwealth of Massachusetts. He touched on Jack Kennedy's presence at the Conference, meeting and interviewing world leaders in attendance for the Hearst news service.

When the column was finished, I delivered it to Charlie Brown at the Western Union press headquarters in the hotel, returned to Bob's room to assure him the column was on the wire and offered to help him contact someone who could repair his glasses, but he preferred to wait until morning because, he said, "I was able to get one lens back in with the help of some Scotch tape and the cracked lens doesn't bother me a bit." He was a sight to behold but appeared able to move about with his makeshift glasses.

Bob wanted to listen to the newscasts on radio in his room to keep abreast of developments at the Conference, so I left him and departed for the lobby, hoping to run into Jack Kennedy. After searching the lobby, I decided to see whether he was in his room. There was no answer. Suddenly, I felt, I would be violating a trust if I mentioned Bob's column to Jack and convinced myself he would hear about it from Boston when *The Post* editions hit the street.

I returned to my room and was getting ready for bed when my phone rang.

It was Bob Norton.

"John," he screamed angrily, "come right over to my room. I'm in a hell of a fix!" When I entered Bob's room he looked downcast.

"Eddie Dunn (the city editor of *The Boston Post*), killed the story on Jack Kennedy and wants another right away," he declared. "He made it damned clear on the phone just now that he wants it on the San Francisco Conference and not Boston politics."

"Guess the old Sarge," as Dunn was known to Boston newspapermen, "checked the story out with Joe Kennedy and he spiked it," Bob reasoned.

He sat on the edge of his bed, his shirt collar open and tie dangling down his front, trying to think of an angle he could cover about the Conference. He had missed two briefings for the press that day and reaped nothing of any consequence from the radio newscasts he heard only a short time before. Suddenly he recalled an old newspaper friend, Peter Edson of Washington, was in the city covering the Conference for Newspaper Enterprises Association.

Reaching for the phone, in a movement of desperation, he

asked the hotel operator to locate Edson for him. In a few minutes he reached his Washington columnist friend, explained his plight and before putting the telephone down, asked me to go to Edson's room on the same floor and "pick up his black sheet," the carbon copy of his column filed that night for publication in the morning newspapers subscribing to the NEA Service.

Edson's only request as he handed me the carbon copy of his column on the Conference was to have Bob change the lead of the story.

When I returned to Bob's room, I read him the column. After he digested the contents for a few minutes, he dictated a new lead and I took the copy to Charlie Brown to be wired to *The Post*. The next day, the Edson column appeared on Page One of *The Post* under the usual heading: "Robert L. Norton comments ... ".

Bob went to bed. So did I, chuckling over the experience of that day.

3

April 1945
Lunch with Jack

At breakfast the following morning, I learned that President Roosevelt, who was scheduled to address the San Francisco Conference on April 25, had left his Hyde Park home to rest at his health resort in Warm Springs, Georgia. Newspapermen in the dining room had mixed reactions to the announcement, and a few mentioned his health. One who had covered the President's report to the joint session of Congress on March 1, on what had been accomplished the month before at the Yalta Conference, expressed the belief that the Yalta trip was a severe drain on the Chief Executive. He took from his pocket a copy of the story he had written on the report to Congress, quoting the President's introduction to his address:

"I hope that you will pardon me for this unusual posture of sitting down during the presentation of what I want to say, but I know that you will realize that it makes it a lot easier for me not to have to carry about ten pounds of steel around the bottom of my legs; and also because of the fact that I have just completed a 14,000-mile trip."

Another newsman commented that he could not recall ever hearing President Roosevelt refer to his crippled legs since

1928 when he was campaigning for election as governor of New York, and at the same time stumping for Al Smith in his bid for the Presidency.

Listening to veteran newspapermen discuss world problems and to study the ways they went about their work was an exciting experience for me. Here I found myself rubbing elbows with reporters from all parts of the world. I thought of the time when I would be discharged from the U.S. Navy and back in the newsroom of *The Berkshire Eagle* in Western Massachusetts. And a plus sign too, I felt, was making the acquaintance of a refreshing personality like Jack Kennedy.

After scanning a newspaper at breakfast, I found my way to the 12th Naval District Headquarters where I produced my orders to the Office of Naval Intelligence, wondering what type of an assignment I would draw. That first day was uneventful as far as ONI was concerned, but I was happy after checking in when a senior officer suggested that I make myself available at the Palace in case there was job I could handle the first day on the job. That left me free to join Jack for lunch at the hotel.

When I met Jack for lunch in the Palm Room of the Palace Hotel, he was with two friends who joined us. In his usual way, he was more interested at the moment in wondering whether the hotel made my room comfortable. Then he introduced me to his friends. The discussion at the table wandered in many directions. Jack's friends were discussing sailing and swimming at Cape Cod. The conversation shifted to foreign dignitaries attending the Conference, none of whom I recognized at the time. Then Jack turned to me and asked: "How did you and Bob make out last night?"

When I described the meeting with General Smuts, Jack beamed; and he almost broke up with laughter when I recited the Norton-Cunningham confrontation at the cocktail party. Anxious to hear how things went at the buffet at the St. Francis Hotel, I tried to emphasize that Bob recuperated pretty well after we got him some food.

"Did Bob get his column off to *The Post?*" Jack asked as my napkin fell to the floor, giving me a moment to answer him.

"Yes," I replied, "he finally sent a good column off, but it took a little doing.

"Why?" Jack wanted to know.

"Well, he experienced a little difficulty in getting the right subject," I answered, blushing and hoping Jack would not notice a flush which suddenly engulfed my face.

Fortunately for me, he accepted the explanation and turned to his friends mentioning that he would be leaving San Francisco the next day and would probably be back in time for President Roosevelt's address.

While sitting there at lunch, I wondered when he would mention the Norton story promoting him as the next mayor of Boston. I was sure Ambassador Kennedy had informed him of the article, believing Bob's story that Mr. Kennedy had killed it. But Jack never mentioned it. I felt almost compelled to tell him, but restrained myself, feeling he will find out about it soon enough.

Jack had left San Francisco before I received word from the Navy that a Board of Medical Survey had determined I was physically qualified for limited, stateside duty, only because of my arthritic condition.

Before he left, Jack left a message at the desk for me, explaining his early departure and a note stating simply, "I'll be in touch." Little did I realize how much he meant it.

The following day I checked in with ONI and happily learned I was assigned to a security staff to check reports on sailors and officers of the Navy thought to be talking too much about their experiences overseas. ONI was concerned with some of the returning Navy personnel who were found to be uttering uncomplimentary remarks about the Japanese and Russians. With so many foreign countries represented at the Conference, tensions were running high and security was tight.

After work one night I went to the Happy Valley Bar in the hotel, hoping to add to my list of newspaperman, and struck up a conversation with a young man sitting on a stool next to me.

At that point, Tony, the bartender approached us.

"Haven't you fellows met?" he asked.

"This is George Vanderbilt," said Tony, "meet John Mahanna."

At first I couldn't believe it, but when I mentioned Lenox, Massachusetts, my birthplace, George turned in amazement and inquired:

"Is Hagyard's drugstore still on the corner?"

Unlike the unexpected meeting with Jack Kennedy, this one gave me a bit more to talk about.

George's mother, Mrs. Margaret Emerson, was the widow of Alfred Gwynne Vanderbilt Jr. George and his brother were students in the first class of the new Lenox School for Boys, an Episcopal institution, when I was a student at Lenox High School.

We saw much of one another while growing up in Lenox. To keep her sons happy, Mrs. Emerson arranged twice weekly to have her chauffeurs drive cars to Lenox proper to pick up boys her sons' ages, take them to her spacious estate, Holmwood, and choose baseball teams among her employees and youngsters to play for about two hours after which the hired help returned to their respective duties. There was no need to bring baseball equipment to the Vanderbilt estate. Mrs. Emerson saw to that. Gloves, shin guards, chest protectors, bats and balls were provided for the teams. After each game, the boys from town were served soft drinks, milk, sandwiches, cakes, cookies and strawberry shortcake, then were driven back to the center o town until a repeat performance two or three days later.

Ironically, I learned George was assigned to ONI in San Francisco at the time. He invited me to visit his office the next day so I could meet a few of the other officers attached to the office. He also invited me to lunch with him the following day when his brother, Alfred, would be in the city. Alfred, I discovered, was commanding officer of a small ship which was docked in the area for repairs.

At lunch we had quite a reunion, reminiscing about our younger days in Lenox and the paths we followed since leaving there. Alfred had to leave that afternoon, but George made a date with me to meet him early that evening in the lobby. He wanted me to meet a friend, a member of the Whitney family, who was hospitalized in the city.

When we met that evening about 7, George, dressed in civilian clothes, was carrying in his arm a tiny Chihuahua, which he said belonged to the Whitney girl. He invited me to accompany him to the hospital, hoping we could smuggle the dog into the elevator and up to her room. I went along with the plan, not knowing the part I was to play would leave a lasting impression. George tucked the dog into the pocket of his raincoat, but the animal started whimpering. Then he asked me to take it, put it in my white-covered officers hat and try to hide it from the staff. Everything worked smoothly until we entered his friend's hospital room and I lifted the frightened dog from my cap, only to discover it apparently was not housebroke and a yellowish stain showed through my cap. We all visited briefly as George's friend caressed the Chihuahua and we made a quick exit. When we returned to the hotel, I went to my room, picked out another white cap cover, turned on the radio and started laughing.

"What a city!" I exclaimed, "never a dull moment!"

Russian ships were anchored offshore in the Bay Area. Newspaper headlines featured stories that the Russians insisted on keeping a communications ship anchored in the bay rather than set up installations ashore.

Rumors circulated throughout the conference that strong objections would be made by other countries about the Soviet policy. Russian sailors were not seen on the streets of San Francisco, although military personnel from other countries were in evidence everywhere.

The war in the Pacific continued at a fast pace as United States forces pressed toward Okinawa heading for the Japanese mainland.

4

April 1945
Talking with Jack about WW II

W hile talking with Jack, my thoughts went back to the stories I had read the year before about his heroism on PT-109 when his craft was cut in two by a Japanese destroyer during the Solomon Islands campaign, but it was obvious he did not want to discuss it in any great detail. His only comment was that "we were lucky to come out of it as well as we did." I sensed then a bit of shyness in his makeup. He shifted the conversation to my experiences in making amphibious landings on atolls in the Pacific and whether I wrote any stories about the engagements with the Japanese.

I told him about writing the ship's history from the time the U.S.S. Heywood was converted to a Navy vessel from the old City of Baltimore, through the battles of Guadalcanal, the Aleutians, Tarawa, Eniwetok, Kwajalein, Saipan, Tinian and finally the D-Day battles in the Philippines when we were part of a task force which returned General MacArthur to Dulag through the Leyte Gulf.

Eyewitness accounts of the landings on atolls in the Marshall Islands, the invasion of the Mariannas and Philippine campaigns which I had written were carried in my newspaper

The Berkshire Eagle back home, I explained, as we discussed the problem of censorship at CINCPAC, Admiral Nimitz's headquarters at Pearl Harbor.

He asked whether we ever operated near PT boat bases and was elated to learn we helped to provision a few.

"We were always on the prowl for food," he said, as I related an experience at Noumea where our departure for the States for ship repairs was delayed while we were transferring part of our experienced crew and landing crafts to other new attack transports for the upcoming attack on Iwo Jima.

While other ships were being provisioned from the Heywood for the assault on Okinawa, a PT boat came alongside one afternoon when I was serving as Officer of the Deck. "Can you spare any food? We're fresh out," a young tanned officer yelled up the gangway over the roar of the PT boat motors.

I summoned the chief commissary steward, Sid Sands, a veteran of 20 years' service in the Navy, to see how we could be of assistance, realizing the captain and executive officer both were ashore.

"What do you need?" asked Sandy, leaning over the gangway.

"Anything you can spare," replied the PT boat officer.

Sandy lost little time in getting a work party together. Fifteen minutes later the deck was covered with crates of oranges, grapefruit, powdered eggs, dehydrated potatoes, turkeys, some canned goods, and enough beef to last the PT crew for some time.

As the boom swung out and the net of provisions was

lowered into the torpedo boat, the skipper inquired: "Anyone from Massachusetts up there?"

The majority of officers and crew on board the Heywood came either from the Midwest or West Coast.

"Guess I'm the only one around here from Massachusetts," I told the young officer.

"Great," he exclaimed, "You must know Jack Kennedy. He's a great guy. I'm from the Old Bay State."

As I tried to catch his name, the motors churned on the PT boat. I heard nothing but a roar as the craft headed out to sea and the crew in chorus waved and smiled with an air of thanks for the handout.

Jack mentioned there were a number of Massachusetts fellows on PT duty in the Pacific. He described them all as "terrific guys."

5

April 12, 1945
Death of FDR

On April 12, 1945 as we were entering the St. Francis Hotel for lunch, the news of President Roosevelt's death was flashed to the nation. We were just walking through the lobby when we noticed everyone appeared to be stunned. The guests were motionless. Some were crying. Desk clerks and bellmen communicated in whispers. A radio in a room nearby was pouring out tribute to the President and carrying bulletins on reactions from leaders around the world. Only solemn music was aired between newscasts. There were no commercials.

We ordered lunch but had lost our appetites. Quietly we left the hotel, returned to the Palace where the shock of Roosevelt's death had its full impact on the members of the press covering the Conference. Soon afterward, Sally returned to Oakland and I to the hospital. We were both too depressed to remain any longer in San Francisco that day.

Following my discharge from the hospital and joining up with ONI, word was received one morning in the communications room that the U.S.S. Intrepid had been damaged by the Japanese somewhere in the Pacific. There were some casualties, according to the secret message. I thought of

Monty who had gone aboard only a few weeks before. "What about Sally?", I thought. My oath prevented me from leaking any information to her or anyone else for that matter. I eagerly checked other reports during the day, hoping to find a casualty list.

One message reported the damaged ship was being returned to the West Coast for repairs. Soon the casualty list was received. Trying not to display my personal interest, I scanned the list of dead and those injured. Monty's name was missing, and I breathed a sigh of relief. It was after the news broke in papers around the city that I confessed to Sally that I had full knowledge of the Intrepid from the time it was hit, and explained my position with ONI which she understood.

6

Spring 1945
Helping a Friend from Italy

I spent the rest of the spring with ONI, investigating routine security cases, occasionally being sent to the docks in Oakland.

My close friend, Ted Giddings, city editor of *The Berkshire Eagle*, in Pittsfield, Massachusetts, mentioned in a letter forwarded to my hotel from my ship that the former social editor of *The Eagle*, Sally Brownell Montanari, was living in Oakland. Her husband, Valerio R. Montanari ("Monty"), who was a city staff reporter on *The Eagle* prior to the war, had been commissioned a lieutenant, junior grade in the Navy and was assigned to the U.S.S. Intrepid, I learned from Ted's letter. San Francisco was the ship's home port.

When we were reporters on the Pittsfield newspaper, Monty and I shared a room at the YMCA. Soon after the outbreak of World War II, Monty sought a commission in the Navy. Despite his credentials as a Harvard graduate and experienced newspaperman, he ran into problems with the Bureau of Naval Personnel.

Monty's cousin, Marshal Pietro Badoglio, was in command of the Italian forces in October 1935 when Italy declared war on France and Great Britain. Adding to his plight was the fact that his brother, Dr. Franco Montanari, was the Italian vice consul in Hawaii, up to the time of the Pearl Harbor attack.

After Hitler's armies invaded Poland in 1939, Italy proclaimed its neutrality. Great Britain and France declared war on Germany. The Russians and Germans in the fall of 1939 arranged to divide Poland between the two countries. The following spring, the Germans occupied Denmark, invaded Norway, Belgium, the Netherlands and Luxembourg. Then Neville Chamberlain resigned as prime minister of Great Britain. A coalition cabinet, including Conservatives and Laborites, was quickly formed, taking office under Winston Churchill.

Monty eagerly followed these events from the newsroom of *The Eagle* during the early months of World War II.

His deep concern didn't surface in the open until June 10, 1940 when in the wire room he read the Associated Press stories that Italy had declared war on France and Great Britain.

He broke down in tears, went back to his desk and wept openly, holding his head in his hands. It was a sad sight.

Only a few close friends knew what was going through his mind.

The telegraph editor, Don Coleman, came to my desk suggesting that I take Monty to our room at the YMCA. After we arrived there, he pleaded with me to stay with him for a while. He said he felt so alone, so depressed and disappointed with the Italian government.

He kept pounding the pillow on his bed, asking, "Why? Why? Why?"

Monty told me that he was sure his cousin, Marshal Badoglio, did not approve of Mussolini's actions. He feared for the safety of his brother, Franco, in Hawaii.

Soon he regained his composure, turned off the radio, stared out the window and turning to me said:

"I need a drink. Let's go to Pat Flynn's."

Pat, a congenial Irishman, operated a neighborhood saloon on a side street in the city, opposite the YMCA. He was a popular figure in Pittsfield, not only as a saloonkeeper and sports fan, but because as a soldier in World War I, he lost a decision in a boxing tournament in Europe as a heavyweight to Gene Tunney, who later became heavyweight champion of the world.

Flynn was a favorite among the newspapermen in the city. As we entered the saloon, we were soon made aware of Pat's feelings about the Italian government declaring war on France and Great Britain. Monty seemed to be oblivious to Pat's outcries as we sat on the stools at the bar. He had known Monty for some time, but not until I called him aside to explain Monty's association through relatives to the Italian government and what had happened in the last hour, did he realize the effect Italy's action had on my friend.

Softening his voice he reached for a bottle of bourbon, placed a glass in front of Monty, half filled it and commanded Monty to down it and have another. "You'll be okay."

Within a short time, Monty showed signs of relaxing a bit, thanked Pat for his kindness and returned with me to our room at the Y where he climbed into bed and fell asleep.

I returned to the newsroom of *The Eagle* to report Monty

was fine and decided to take a nap, but would not be back at his desk until the next morning.

The next day he resumed covering his City Hall beat, comforted by the fact that his colleagues and city officials whom he met daily, were sympathetic or refrained entirely from discussing with him Italy's role in the war.

In the newsroom Monty continued to keep a constant eye on the AP machine, read the *New York Times*, the *Christian Science Monitor* and all of the Boston newspapers to follow the latest developments in Europe.

In our room at the Y he listened constantly to radio newscasts until he retired for the night.

Later in the fall of 1940 he became aroused again when Germany, Italy and Japan concluded a three-power pact at Berlin, pledging total mutual aid to all members for a period of 10 years.

Monty and I had registered for military service under the Selective Service Act, but were not classified for some time. We discussed volunteering rather than waiting to be drafted. We began exploring leads to obtain commissions in the military services.

Both of us favored the U.S. Navy.

In the meantime, there were other developments affecting Monty's cousin, General Badoglio. Soon after Hitler and Mussolini conferred in Florence, Italian forces launched an attack in October upon Greece. General Badoglio, who had resisted joining Hitler's war, resigned as chief of staff following reverses suffered by the Italian armies attacking Greece.

The deteriorating relations between the United States and Italy were forcefully brought home to Monty in a most personal way when, in June 1941, Under Secretary of State Sumner Welles "requested" the Italian Ambassador, at the direction of President Roosevelt, to close all Italian consulates within U.S. territory and withdraw all their officers and employees by July 15.

The Italian consulate in Honolulu was duly closed. Monty's brother, Franco, took a ship to San Francisco and a train to New York, where he was supposed to promptly board another ship, along with other Italian and German officials, for Europe. But Franco could not see returning to Italy — with a war in Europe which could jump the oceans at any time — without at least a glimpse of his American, indeed, proper Bostonian-born, mother, then living in Stowe, Vermont, and his Italian born brother, Monty, who had derived U.S. citizenship from their mother.

Some rather frantic bilingual telephone calls from New York to diplomatic friends, including one of Monty's Harvard classmates in Washington shortly before his ship was to leave for Europe, enabled Franco to miss the sailing, and visit his mother in Vermont and his brother in Lenox, Massachusetts.

Proud of his brother despite the official heavy clouds over him, Monty arranged with a news friend, Bob Burbank, for his brother to be interviewed over WBRK in Pittsfield — but not on war-related subjects at Franco's request. After all, he had been allowed to stay on beyond his deadline, and did not wish to embarrass those who had arranged it.

Monty traveled by train to New York with Franco and with a

heavy heart said goodbye at dockside. He would not see his brother again for some eight years, including several years when they technically were "enemies."

Monty gloomily read reports of the gradual domination of Italy by the German Nazis. When a baby, he had lost his father, an Italian general and member of the Italian General Staff, who was killed on the Austrian front during World War I, and now he was naturally fearful for his brother's safety.

The events of the next ensuing period, including the Japanese surprise attack on Pearl Harbor and the United States declaration of war on Japan, Germany and Italy, were nervously followed by Monty who was unable to communicate with his brother in Italy.

Against this background of events in Europe, the Navy turned down Monty's application for a commission and accepted his enlistment instead. After boot training in Newport, Rhode Island, and technical training at the Naval Air Station at Jacksonville, Florida, he served as an aviation radioman-gunner and trainer.

While he was in Jacksonville, I was accepted by the Navy as a warrant boatswain, specialist, assigned by the First Naval District as an investigator with the Office of Naval Intelligence, working out of a regional office in Springfield, Massachusetts.

One morning I was handed a security check case by my superior officer at ONI — "Subject: Valerio Riccardo Montanari, Pittsfield, Massachusetts."

Amused that I should draw an assignment to check on my old friend, I realized that, although I knew him personally, it would be necessary to do a complete investigation, interviewing others who knew him and verifying the information contained in his case file. I could attest to his patriotism, honesty, and loyalty to the United States. He had lived in this country most of his life. To my knowledge he never had a blemish on his record. He was a citizen of the United States. His sister was the manager of a private home for wayward children in Boston. On his mother's side he had reputable relatives living in the Boston area, whose forebears were early settlers a few years after the Mayflower landed at Plymouth.

His official papers revealed he was being considered for an appointment in the U.S. Navy as a lieutenant, junior grade. When the investigation was completed without turning up any derogatory information, I filed the report. However, before any action was taken by the Bureau of Naval Personnel, I was transferred to the Navy Indoctrination School for officers at the University of Arizona in Tucson, then to gunnery school in La Jolla, California and finally to the U.S.S. Heywood, an attack transport, in the South Pacific. It wasn't until many months later I learned Monty had been accepted.

It was not until after the war that Monty learned of the important part his brother, Franco, had played in Italy's surrender. In July 1943 — after the arrest of Mussolini — their cousin, Marshal Badoglio, formed a new government and began secret overtures for surrender. Because of his American relationship and because he knew him and trusted him, Badoglio chose Franco as one of two officials for a secret and dangerous mission to Lisbon to discuss surrender. It was a real cloak-and-dagger exploit under the noses of numerous German spies, involving secret night meetings at the home of the British Ambassador to Portugal. But that's another story.

When I succeeded in locating Monty's wife, Sally, in Oakland, I was still a patient at Treasure Island Naval Hospital. She informed me that Monty had been commissioned a lieutenant, junior grade and was aboard the U.S.S. Intrepid, having left the port at San Francisco a short time before I arrived in the same port aboard the U.S.S. Heywood.

The letter from Ted Giddings, which I received several days later, included the same information. Monty's promotion and assignment took me back to the days I investigated Monty, and for the first time I told Sally about it.

Sally filled me in on her activities in San Francisco. She had a job with the National Broadcasting Company at the San Francisco Conference, doing everything from fetching hot dogs and coffee for radio commentators like H. T. Kaltenborn and Richard Harkness, to escorting around the city such personalities as the well-known hostess, Elsa Maxwell.

Sally was living in Oakland, across the Bay, at the home of her cousins, Jack and Marion Henry. Jack, a doctor in the Navy, had been ordered to the Atlantic Fleet and his wife had gone to New York to be near him. Both were happy to have someone like Sally living in their home.

A few hours after telephoning Sally at her cousins' home, she appeared at the admissions desk of Treasure Island Naval Hospital, inquiring about my health and requesting to see me. I was in bed reading when an orderly entered my room to inform me that I had a visitor.

Grabbing my robe, I followed him to the visitor's waiting

room where Sally leaped from a chair, ran into my arms and asked, "Are you OK?"

Although I was not aware of it, the senior medical officer of the hospital, Commodore Stanley, was observing the greeting. When I saw him smiling at this reunion with the first person I had met from Pittsfield since leaving home two years before, I introduced him to Sally, providing a brief description of our long-standing friendship.

Sally, an exhilarating person, lost no time in asking Dr. Stanley the general condition of my health and whether I had to remain confined for long.

"Why, John may leave the hospital anytime during the day after he takes care of his tests and therapy," he replied, "but he must stick to a schedule we have set up for him for a few days."

"Well, what are we waiting for?" exclaimed Sally. "Get dressed. I'm on my way to San Francisco and want to show you some of the city and meet a few of my friends."

Losing little time in getting back to the ward, I hurriedly put on my uniform. When I reached the visitor's lounge, I found Sally and the commodore sitting on a bench laughing, obviously enchanted over some story one or the other had just related.

"Come on, John," said Sally as she directed me to the front door of the hospital, "the commodore is giving us a lift in his staff car to the Palace Hotel. He's going right past there."

Outside, a Marine sergeant snapped a salute as the commodore emerged, then opened both doors of the sedan for us to enter. Dr. Stanley rode in the front. As we drove over the

Oakland Bay Bridge, we learned the commodore was a writer too. Before the war, he was senior medical officer at San Quentin Prison. While there he authored a book, *Men at Their Worst*, but now was working on another, *Men at Their Best*, based on his experiences with injured Navy personnel from the war in the Pacific.

"Don't stay out too late, John," said the commodore, smiling as we arrived at the side entrance to the Palace Hotel. "Try to be back at the hospital by 9 and have a good time," he added as we thanked him for the ride into the city. With that kind of a schedule handed to me, Sally and I agreed we would be able to see each other in the next few days if her duties with NBC at the San Francisco Conference could be arranged to allow for a lunch or dinner.

From left to right: Dorothy (wife of Joe DiMaggio), their son Joe Jr., Joe DiMaggio, John G. W. Mahanna, his wife Evona, and their daughter, Joan.

7

1945
A Vacation with Joe DiMaggio

Soon after spring, the Navy informed me that a board of medical survey had determined that, due to my arthritic condition, I was physically qualified for limited duty only.

Released from active duty with an honorable discharge, I headed back to my home in Pittsfield.

Before returning to my newspaper post at *The Eagle*, Evona had arranged a vacation for us with our three-year-old daughter, Joan, at Lake Champlain in Vermont.

She chose a quiet resort, the Basin Harbor Club, near Vergennes. After registering we inspected the surroundings, four tennis courts, a golf course, boating, swimming and other attractions including movies and beano (bingo) games.

At dinner the first night we noticed an absence of young people among the guests in the dining room. Adjusting to this atmosphere with elderly people all around us after San Francisco was a trifle difficult at first. On our second day, however, the picture changed when we noticed another couple our age seated at the far end of the dining room with a boy about Joan's age.

The children were first to meet as they romped around the

dining room tables. That brought us together with Joe DiMaggio, the great Yankee baseball star and his wife, the former Dorothy Arnold and their son, Joe Jr. Joe had recently been discharged from the U.S. Army and like ourselves wanted to spend a few days quietly in the hills of Vermont.

A quick friendship developed after we learned junior hostesses were available to care for the children, giving us an opportunity to play golf and enjoy other forms of entertainment at the resort.

On the golf course, Joe's power as a baseball slugger showed up off the tees. He was a long ball hitter to be sure, but his long drives at times failed to stay on the fairways. His slice usually ended up in a thick forest of trees. After a few days, however, the tips he received from his wife, Dorothy, an accomplished golfer, helped to improve his game.

The DiMaggios had traveled by air to Vermont and were without an automobile. One morning Joe decided he wanted to see more of the countryside and we provided the transportation in our car. We went to Burlington for lunch. Although, due to his war service (DiMaggio enlisted in the United States Army Air Forces on February 17, 1943) he had been out of a Yankee baseball uniform for some time, he was quickly recognized when we entered a small restaurant on a side street.

Pedestrians who saw him enter the place peered through the plate glass windows from the street as we were seated at a table. Soon waitresses and customers came over seeking autographs which he graciously gave to them.

But, try as he might to seek a little privacy, Joe felt he could only escape the limelight back at the resort in his small cabin on the shores of Lake Champlain.

En route back to Basin Harbor we stopped at a state liquor store, purchased a bottle of bourbon and settled down in the quiet of his cabin to enjoy cocktails before dinner that night, far from the eyes of the public.

That evening, the feature event at the resort was a square dance in one of the red barns on the property. The caller, a typical Vermonter, with his fiddle and a trip of musicians, explained that square dancing was easy to learn, encouraging everyone to take part. He had difficulty at first in getting enough couples on the floor to form a square, but finally managed to get sixteen couples to participate in two groups. Joe and I were not among them, but our wives responded with enthusiasm. Both had square danced before.

Standing like wallflowers at the edge of the dance floor, Joe and I applauded their moves as they followed the instructions of the caller. When it became time for other groups to join in, Evona persuaded Joe to join her group and I followed Dorothy on to the dance floor in another group.

We went through the motions — or tried to follow the calls — but at times reversed our positions causing collisions with our partners, but our tolerant friends appeared to enjoy it.

A baseball game was scheduled the next day with teams selected by the resort management from among the guests. Because of his professional standing, it was explained, Joe's name was missing from the rosters, but he was asked to umpire.

I was named the starting pitcher for our team. When I went to the mound, Joe positioned himself at my back. While warming up, he reminded me of the rules of the game, limiting me to the number of pitches I could throw in a warmup. With deadpan seriousness, he inspected my glove and pulled his fingers through my hair to see if I was using any foreign substance for "a sinker or curve ball."

When I threw the first pitch, he announced "ball" before it hit the catcher's mitt. He warned my angry teammates to control their tempers after he allowed a base on balls to each of the first three batters I faced.

The fourth batsman bunted, fell running to first and our catcher tagged the runner going home from third base, then threw to the third baseman where two runners were standing on the bag. When they stepped off the bag the third baseman tagged both of them and then threw to first before the fallen bunter reached the sack.

"Four outs," I yelled at Joe as he tried to reconstruct this weird picture. "Only three is necessary in this game," he replied, doubling up in laughter.

As the game wore on, Joe was enjoying it as much as the players and spectators. It ended in a tie.

Evona, Joan, and I drove the DiMaggios to Burlington the next morning where they boarded a plane for New York. A few days later we returned to Pittsfield.

8

1947 and 1948
Reconnecting with JFK

G etting back into newspaper work was an exciting experience. My return came just in time to cover the local area reaction to the surrender of the Japanese in the Pacific in August 1945.

Then, not too long after, I read in a Boston newspaper one morning that Jack Kennedy was entering politics. It came as a surprise to me at first because in looking back on our meeting in San Francisco, I was left with the impression that he would pursue a career in writing.

Reflecting on our conversations in the Palace Hotel, I recalled his intense interest in my stories about my experience as a political reporter before the war. I began to think that underneath his inquisitiveness about politicians I had known and covered, he must have had a strong, compelling urge to enter the political arena and abandon journalism. Apparently it was a vision he shared with no one at the time.

After Jack won the special 1946 election in the 11th Massachusetts District, we met again in his congressional office in Washington in 1947 during one of our visits with Evona's family in Georgetown.

The happy reunion at lunch in the Congressional Hotel, adjacent to his office in the Cannon House Office Building, gave us an opportunity to review our activities since we parted in San Francisco two years before.

Jack looked terribly thin. He had a yellowish complexion but his sense of humor erased any feelings one would have about his health. He was enthusiastic about his new role in Congress. He seemed to be unaffected, sincere and self-assured in his new surroundings.

He wanted to get better known outside of Boston, especially in the western part of the state. Apparently he had his sights on a statewide office such as the governorship, U.S. Senate or even the Presidency.

My role, he explained, because of my newspaper connections in Western Massachusetts was to get him speaking engagements wherever I could, regardless of the size of the audience. He wanted exposure in areas where, he felt, the Kennedy name was not too well known.

He indicated he would like to visit us in Western Massachusetts sometime after Congress adjourned, but I did not take him seriously at the time. Less than a year later, however, he contacted me at the newsroom of *The Eagle*. He asked me to meet him on March 22, 1948 in North Adams, where he had accepted an invitation to address the North Adams Aerie of Eagles at a father-son dinner.

After getting filled in on his schedule — his first trip to the Berkshires, the westernmost county in the Commonwealth — I met him late on the afternoon of March 22 on the steps of the Richmond Hotel.

Expecting this wealthy young congressman to arrive in a luxurious limousine, I found him riding in a beat-up sedan spattered with mud. He was accompanied by Bob Morey, his chauffeur (a young Bostonian and former boxer), and Frank Morrissey, his secretary, who handled his schedules out of his Boston office. From that time on, Morrissey and Morey, made many more trips back to Western Massachusetts with the young Congressman to fill engagements I had arranged for him throughout the area.

Jack's first request that day was for a quick fill-in on the city — its industries, politics, people, government officials, schools, colleges and anything else I could think of to give him a feel of this community of about 23,000 people.

The shyness I had seen in him before seemed to have lessened as he would politely excuse himself from our conversation to introduce himself to the hotel doorman, bellhops, guests in the lobby or anyone else within reach of a handshake.

During this visit, I began to visualize the ground-level technique he wanted developed along the way to make his appearances as personal as possible. It was here I discovered one of the secrets of his success as a politician — the human touch.

I observed Frank Morrissey with pad and pencil approach each person Jack met, copy down their names and addresses and note the subject of their conversation, and the place it took place. I found myself doing the same thing from that time on.

Later I learned the names and addresses were quickly relayed to the congressman's Boston office, sometimes by telephone if his visit extended beyond a day. His Boston staff prepared personal letters mentioning the meeting, and the individuals usually received a "personal" letter from the young congressman soon after they had met him.

Jack never carried a personal card to hand out to newfound friends. He depended on those around him to make sure they knew who he was talking with. He had a way of making people feel he was interested in their problems be it a policeman complaining about low salaries, a housewife up in arms over taxes or the cost of living, a town or city official seeking guidance on obtaining flood control funds, or a civic leader in a small community seeking help in acquiring a Civil War cannon for the Village Green.

After our meeting in North Adams to discuss his future plans, I told him the story of Bob Norton and James Michael Curley. He loved it.

9

1950
Political Strategy in the Berkshires

J ack's North Adams trip resulted in speculation among many
political observers, both the professionals and street corner
types, as to whether Jack had his eyes on the governor's seat.
Others predicted he just wanted to get on a statewide ballot for
a lesser office such as lieutenant governor or secretary of the
Commonwealth, in order to become better known and build his
fences to become chief executive of the commonwealth.

Jack was not happy with the makeup of the Democratic
State Committee or the Democrats in power at the State House.

From the outset of his "visits" to the rural areas of Western
Massachusetts, he stayed clear of the organized Democratic
committees in the small cities and towns. Whenever I
scheduled a speaking engagement for him, whether it was at a
Holy Name Society communion breakfast, a talk before a local
service club like Rotary or Kiwanis, or as a panel member of
the Workshop for World Understanding, he turned down offers
to attend a Democratic committee meeting, but, if time
permitted, he agreed at times to have a party leader in a
community drop by his hotel on a "courtesy call."

In the early 1950s Roger Linscott, a top-grade reporter on

The Berkshire Eagle, wrote a series of articles on the Massachusetts political scene, which I thought would interest Jack. He had asked me many times to keep in touch with him about happenings in the western part of the state, which might escape his attention in Boston or Washington.

On March 2, 1950, he acknowledged receipt of my letter with the Linscott clippings, mentioning, among other things:

"I enjoyed reading those articles by Roger Linscott because they gave me some local information about that section that I never heard."

Because of rumors spreading through the area that Jack was seriously considering running for governor, I asked him about it in my letter.

"In your letter you asked about whether I was going to run for Governor this year," he replied. "Speaking to you personally, I do not think that I will, but would rather wait until 1952. I think you will understand why.

"I am planning to spend some time up in that section of the state when Congress adjourns and am looking forward to sitting down with you for a long talk."

At the same time Congressman John Heselton of Greenfield, a Republican serving the First Congressional District, geographically the largest in the state, was seeking re-election in 1950 against a strong Democratic candidate. As a reporter, covering politics for *The Eagle*, I became impressed with Congressman Heselton's record in Washington, and expressed to Jack my hope that he would win in November.

"I agree with you that it would be very unfortunate to see John Heselton beaten," Jack wrote, adding: "He is the best type of representative — conscientious and hard-working — and that is certainly the type that is wanted in politics, regardless of party affiliation."

The City of Pittsfield had just elected a 28-year-old mayor, a Navy veteran, lawyer and son of a veteran state legislator, Robert T. Capeless, whose fresh, youthful approach to local problems seemed to fit into the type Jack Kennedy was urging to enter politics from the ranks of capable young people.

I filled him in on this new young personality on the political scene in Pittsfield and he replied that "I have heard a lot about Bob Capeless and this summer I hope that you will introduce me to him."

I did, and then Bob became an active supporter of Jack Kennedy in the next few years.

10

Spring 1950
Lining up Speaking Engagements

L ater in March 1950, Jack expressed a desire to return to Berkshire County and asked me to start lining up some speaking engagements.

My first thought was to try and place him before a labor group, since he was a member in the House of the Education and Labor Committee.

Then it occurred to me that it would be best to discuss Jack's request with the Rev. Eugene F. Marshall, pastor of St. Mary's, the Morning Star, Catholic Church. Father Marshall, a native of Worcester, and the most influential priest in the city, had strong ties with the labor groups at the General Electric Company. Most of his parishioners in the Morningside section of the city were GE employees.

When I suggested to Father Marshall, that Jack would be available that spring to speak in Pittsfield, he jumped at the opportunity and asked whether I thought it could be arranged before St. Mary's Holy Name Society after Easter, in April or May.

Congress was still in session when the invitation reached the congressman in Washington.

"I am afraid my schedule for those two months is filled up; and the first free Sunday I have is June 4th," Jack wrote, and "if Father Marshall would like me to come on that date, I'll be glad to do so. However, if he feels that he would have to hold the breakfast on an earlier date, I shall understand. In the latter event, perhaps I can get up there after Congress has adjourned."

After discussing Jack's letter with Father Marshall, he conferred with Harold V. Keegan, president of the Holy Name Society. Both agreed to delay the communion breakfast until June 4 when Jack could address the group.

In a letter dated, April 21, 1950, Jack wrote:

"Today I received the invitation from Mr. Harold V. Keegan, President of the Holy Name Society of St. Mary's and have replied that I would be most happy to accept it. I didn't have an opportunity to meet Bob Capeless when he came to Washington recently because of the Easter recess, but I hope to meet him soon, possibly at the breakfast. I'm enclosing, herewith, a glossy photograph and a biographical sketch, which will, I hope, be of some use to you."

The wheels were set in motion for the congressman's first visit to the county seat of the Berkshires, Pittsfield. I prepared news releases for *The Eagle* and the two radio stations in the city, announcing his upcoming visit. Our correspondence after that centered on plans for his short visit. He asked me to make reservations for him at the Hotel Sheraton on the night of June 3, and "be sure to get a hair mattress and bed board." In one of my letters, I asked if he would agree to have dinner at our home and meet a few friends from my newspaper, as well as the Mayor and Mrs. Capeless.

"Any sort of a get-together which you would like to hold would meet with my approval," he wrote.

After the press notices of his June 4 appearance appeared in the area newspapers, a few local politicians started to move in on the visit but when they contacted me about his schedule, I could only reply that it was "pretty tight, but I'll see if we can arrange some time for you to meet the congressman."

Jack had made it clear he was not coming to the Berkshires on a "political tour." I was at a loss as to what to do. After contacting Frank Morrissey at his Boston office, I was assured he would handle the visits with the area politicians when they arrived.

Unknown to me, one of the county's politicians, James P. McAndrews of Adams, a former state senator and unsuccessful candidate for Congress in the First District, had written to Jack in Washington, inviting him to a dinner.

On May 9, 1950, I received this letter from Jack, marked PERSONAL AND CONFIDENTIAL:

"With regard to my coming to Pittsfield on June 4th, I have received an invitation from Jim McAndrews of Adams to attend a little dinner party the night before I speak, or the following night.

"He intends to gather together a small group who might be helpful to me in the event I go statewide at some future date. Knowing of some of the confusion in the local picture, I wondered if it would be advisable for me to attend such a dinner.

"Could you check on this and let me know immediately?"

I advised the congressman that it would be better to pass up the invitation at the time because if he accepted one, it would be difficult to explain to others why he could not honor them with his presence.

"Thank you for your letter of May 11," he wrote, "I have taken your advice about the dinner, and hope to be able to make it to Adams sometime after the adjournment of Congress.

"I note in your letter that WBEC plans to carry my talk on June 4th. I had not thought that my address would be broadcast, and in view of that fact had planned to talk very informally. If my address is broadcast it would be necessary for me to make a prepared speech, and I don't think it would be as satisfactory as an informal talk. If the manager of the radio station could cancel his arrangements to broadcast the speech I would appreciate it. However, if all arrangements have definitely been made, and it would disrupt things to cancel the time now, then I shall let the broadcast stand."

I went to the Hotel Sheraton on the afternoon of Saturday, June 3 to await the arrival of Congressman Kennedy from Boston. At about 4 he arrived in a sedan, driven by Bob Morey and accompanied by Frank Morrissey with a briefcase under his arm. It was not the Cadillac or Lincoln I had expected to see pull up alongside the curb, but an unpolished, mud-spattered dented vehicle that must have been seven or eight years old.

When he stepped from the automobile a large crowd gathered at the entrance to the hotel to greet him. Shyly he shook hands with many as he walked toward the lobby where the hotel manager, John Donegan, welcomed him and assured him everything was in readiness in his suite.

After he was settled in his quarters, the telephone began to ring. Frank took the calls. They were for the most part from Democratic committee members in the city seeking an appointment with the congressman.

Frank arranged for a few to visit the suite, explaining in each case that the congressman was pressed for time and had to make several official calls before going on to his next appointment, which was dinner with my newspaper friends.

At the dinner at the home of Evona's mother, Mrs. Edward A. Kennedy — with whom we were living at the time with our eight-year-old daughter, Joan and three-year-old son, Jonathan — Jack appeared to be relaxed all evening, enjoying the conversations with my family and friends, but later at night he got up from his chair, excused himself from our guests and asked me to join him on the porch.

There I discovered he had an allergy to dogs. The presence in the house of the family Boston bulldog seemed to affect him. He asked if I could locate a doctor any place. It was near midnight and I recalled that our family physician, Dr. Antonio Desautels, usually spent his Saturday nights at the Franco-American Club which he headed.

Without further delay, I explained to Evona that Jack was not feeling well and wanted to go to his hotel. With that he excused himself from the gathering until I reached Dr. Desautels at the club and asked him if I could go to his office, which was nearby, so he could see Congressman Kennedy who needed some type of medicine.

In a few minutes we met the doctor at his office. Jack

explained his allergy to Dr. Desautels who reached into his cabinet of medicines, poured out some pills in an envelope and gave him instructions on the dosage he should take.

We drove back to the hotel, and visited for a few minutes in his room while Jack prepared for bed. Before I left he assured me he was feeling better and would see me at the hotel first thing in the morning.

When I arrived at the hotel, Jack was in the lobby, looking rested, and volunteered "the pills worked fine and I feel much better." Then we left for St. Mary's Church to attend the 8 a.m. Mass, and afterward went to the Parish Hall for the communion breakfast.

In his address, the congressman assailed this country's China policy, describing it as a "complete failure," and warned that Indochina is the front on which the cold war may be won or lost.

For the present, he said, the Soviet Union apparently does not want war — but, he warned, this is because the Communists have been winning victories without it. As in China, he said, Russian policy is to support armed revolt by native Communist forces.

On the domestic front, he described as "most encouraging, the increasing interest of younger men in seeking national office." He pointed out that "the average age of a congressman is now in the 40s whereas before World War II it was 52 to 53."

"This will be particularly important in future years," he added, "in bringing younger and more active men into the forefront on congressional committees."

Listing the chairmen of key committees, the 33-year-old

congressman, noted that "one is 87 years old, another is 84 and several are in the late 70s." He warned, however, that regardless of younger blood in the Congress, progressive policies will be difficult to put across as long as the present alliance of conservative Southern Democrats and Republicans continues.

This alliance, he declared, has blocked progressive action in many committees where the Democrats are nominally in a majority.

"It is consequently in danger of placing on the party as a whole the stigma of Dixiecrat policies," he concluded.

Following the Holy Name Society's appearance at St. Mary's, Jack was informed there was another communion breakfast going on at Mount Carmel Church Holy Name Society, made up of Italian parishioners.

"Let's go," he said, "I would like to drop by there."

When he entered the hall he was recognized immediately and given a standing ovation. He spoke briefly and we left for his hotel room where he made a few calls to a few civic, business, and labor leaders in the area, and then he returned to Washington.

11

1951 and 1952
Laying the Groundwork

During the first half of 1951, Jack continued to make as many appearances throughout the state as time would permit from his congressional duties in Washington.

He kept in touch with his friends, which were now mounting in the central and western parts of the commonwealth.

In August 1951 he sent me a copy of a bill he was introducing in the House, hoping to get some detailed coverage in the local newspaper and on radio newscasts.

"As you will note," he wrote, "the bill calls for the establishment of a commission, similar to the Hoover Commission, to improve the selection of candidates for the Military and Naval Academies. I am sure you will find it self-explanatory.

"I am likewise sending you a copy of an article which, with some minor changes, will be published in *The New York Times Sunday Magazine* section in next Sunday's edition, August 19, as well as a copy of an article by Mr. Arthur Krock, which appeared in *The New York Times* on Thursday, August 9th.

"I think that our present method of picking cadets and

midshipman has been extremely haphazard, and I think that we have paid and will continue to pay a heavy price for our failure to modernize our techniques.

"I thought that if this matter interested you, you might find some material for an editorial."

On another occasion in 1951, Jack mailed me a copy of a news release announcing that:

"For the first time in history a member of the United States Congress has been awarded the Star of Solidarity the First Order, the highest honor that the Italian government can bestow. Congressman John F. Kennedy of the 11th congressional district."

The release, a lengthy one, told of the Congressman's "constant labors for Americans of Italian extraction," the demand he made on the floor of the House for immediate aid for Italy, the high tribute he paid to Premier Alcide De Gasperi, the resolution he introduced in Congress to relieve the government of Italy of all obligations to the United States under the provisions of the Treaty of Peace with Italy and his "personal efforts to induce Secretary of State Dean Acheson to support such a course of action."

It further explained that Congressman Kennedy was in the forefront of the effort to provide a special measure by Congress to permit five Catholic nuns, who staff the Home for Aged Italians in East Boston, to remain in the United States, and that he was head of a Congressional committee in the move to have President Truman revise the Italian Peace Treaty "and appeared before the President personally in an effort to bring this about."

After Jack introduced in Congress the resolution to relieve

Italy of all obligations in the United States, I found upon my return from work one evening my garage filled with about 25 cardboard cartons of copies of the resolution, with a letter from Jack's Washington office asking me to distribute them to Italian-American organizations in the area and "home delivery," if possible, in the Italian-American section of the city.

Following a brief holiday vacation at the close of 1951, Jack notified me that he was ready to cover more ground in the western part of the state. I arranged a tour early in February 1952, which took him through a number of small towns in the southern part of the Berkshires, an area he had not visited before, highlighted by an appearance in Pittsfield as a member of a panel at the Workshop for World Understanding meeting, an organization sponsored by a group of local residents whose aim was to conduct periodically a Court of Public Opinion on important issues.

The subject discussed that evening was on the question:

"How do Communism, Imperialism, Nationalism and Economic Forces influence American foreign policy and objectives in the Far East?"

In his remarks, Congressman Kennedy told the audience of more than 500 in the auditorium of Pittsfield High School, that "Communists will conquer Indochina unless the French are willing to make concessions to the natives," but even so, he advocated support of the French in Indochina in the event of a Chinese invasion, with a naval blockade and air support.

Jack shared the panel with a Vienna-born Jesuit missionary, the Rev. John A. Walchars of Cranwell Preparatory School in

Lenox, who served eight years in the Far East; Dr. T. W. Liao, a General Electric Company engineer in Pittsfield, who spent 28 years in China; Williams College Professor Fred Greene and Gerald White Jr., of Cedarhurst, N.Y., a resident of China for two-and-one-half years.

Before leaving on his tour of towns in South Berkshire the next morning, Jack, as was always his custom, visited the newsroom of *The Berkshire Eagle*, chatted with the publishers, editors and reporters and before leaving the building walked through the composing room, stopping at each of the Linotype machines to talk with the operators, then watched the make-up men at work and ended his tour on the bottom floor studying every move of the stereotype men working on forms before placing the cylinder on the presses.

He ended the long day and returned to his Pittsfield hotel after midnight, having visited the smaller towns south of the city, the Franco-American, Polish-American, Italian-American Clubs, the homes of the Elks and Eagles, and he jokingly complained "too bad there isn't an Ancient Order of Hibernian Hall here."

Before retiring we sat in his suite for a short time discussing the areas covered that day. Jack kicked off his loafers, took off his tie, ordered a bottle of beer and a cigar, slumped in his chair, completely relaxed and quite satisfied with Kennedy vs. Lodge.

As Jack continued his swing back through Western Massachusetts, he was quick on sight to recognize people he had met on other visits.

The young congressman had a great memory for faces and

names, calling many by their first names but seldom his elders, outside of intimate friends. It was always "Mr." or "Mrs.".

Many who had received personal letters from him after a previous tour through the area never hesitated to let him know how much they appreciated his thoughtfulness. As he walked the streets of the towns, people compared his memory with that of Jim Farley, the one-time chairman of the Democratic National Committee and Postmaster General under President Franklin D. Roosevelt. It was one of Jack's greatest assets in campaigning. The sincerity behind it all created a contagious enthusiasm among people for the young man from Boston.

One night after a speaking engagement in Westfield, while driving the 35 miles over a darkened, mountainous highway, I tried again to find out whether Jack was planning soon to announce his candidacy for governor or U.S. senator.

It was obvious from his stepped-up activity that he had made up his mind to run for a statewide office.

Huddled in the back seat of his sedan with a pillow behind his head and a blanket around his shoulders, he thought for a moment as I posed the question. He didn't want to commit himself to the press just yet, but straightening up in his seat he looked at me and said:

"John, speaking to you personally as a friend, and not for publication, I can't see myself sitting up there in the governor's office in the State House on Beacon Hill in Boston. Those steps up to the State House are filled every day with people and politicians trying to get into the governor's office. There are just too many people. I would never have a minute's peace.

"I couldn't do a good job in that confusion and atmosphere.

If the State House were located someplace else, like in Worcester or between Springfield and Worcester, it might make a difference. New York State had the right idea when the State House was located in Albany. Can you imagine what it would be like if the New York State capitol was in the heart of Manhattan?"

That answered part of my question.

It was not long thereafter, however, that the announcement came from Boston that Jack would seek the Democratic nomination for the U.S. Senate to oppose the incumbent, Senator Henry Cabot Lodge, who was seeking re-election and at the same time serving as General Dwight D. Eisenhower's campaign manager for the Presidency.

12

1952
Campaign for the U.S. Senate

In all the years I had known Jack, he seldom showed signs of being irritated, but in February 1952, I received from him a handwritten letter from his family's home on North Ocean Boulevard, Palm Beach, Florida, spelling out his wrath over a news story which appeared in *The Berkshire Eagle*, criticizing him for his stand on Israel at the time.

The story was written by Edward J. Michelson, a Pittsfield native and a correspondent in Washington for *The Berkshire Eagle*.

Jack's handwriting was something to behold, and in this letter he apparently was angered, writing at top speed.

"It was obvious to me that the story was worked out by Michelson in conjunction with Lodge," the letter began. "The reference to Dad living in Florida being an isolationist, my supposed anti-Israel amendment, and Lodge having trees planted in Israel.

"I'm going to get Michelson and demand he retract the statement ... It is a lie and I'm going to make him eat it." As the campaign started to take shape, Jack's office in Boston asked me to supply a list of names in the two cities and 30 towns in the Berkshires — names of persons who might be interested in serving as the local "secretaries" for the Kennedy-for-Senator Committee. Practically all of the names submitted were people Jack had met during his many tours through the area and none were identified with machine or party politics. They were amateurs in the game.

When the Jefferson-Jackson Day fundraising dinner came around, I was invited to attend by Jack's secretary, Frank Morrissey, who explained he had 10 of the $100-a-plate dinner tickets for a few of the congressman's friends. He instructed me to pick up my ticket at the congressman's apartment at 122 Bowdoin Street, next to the State House, after I arrived in Boston.

When I arrived at the apartment, Jack was going over the speech he was to deliver that night, his first big exposure since announcing his candidacy. At the head table were Governor Paul A. Dever, former Mayor James Michael Curley, statewide Democrat office holders, and others.

At the Copley Plaza Hotel, I found my numbered ticket placed me at a table with nine other young men who had worked closely with Jack ever since he was elected to Congress in Curley's former district. The table was located immediately in front of the speaker's platform.

On another visit to Boston with Evona, the congressman asked us to stop by his apartment to discuss his schedule and plans he had in mind for the campaign. When we arrived at 122 Bowdoin Street, Jack's housekeeper greeted us as she was leaving for a neighborhood grocery store. She explained Jack was taking a shower and would be ready in a few minutes. We made ourselves comfortable in the small living room, when suddenly Jack appeared in the doorway leading to a bedroom.

He had on a white shirt and tie, shorts, socks and shoes, with two pairs of trousers draped over each arm. One was brown, the other black.

"Hi, Evona and John," he said standing before us, "sure glad you could stop by. I have to go a dinner later and I don't know which suit to wear. What do you think, Evona?"

Because of a dinner, Evona suggested the black suit would be better and he entered the bedroom, pulling the black trousers over his legs and tossed the other on his bed.

In a few minutes he emerged, immaculately dressed and we sat down to visit for a short time until he had to leave for his engagement.

It was during this meeting that Jack explained a plan to conduct throughout the state a series of tea parties to attract women supporters. He asked Evona if she would be chairman of the tea parties in the Berkshires. She agreed and within a short time she met with Polly Fitzgerald, wife of Eddie Fitzgerald, a cousin of the Kennedys, who outlined the plans to invite area women to meet the congressman, his mother and sisters to tea.

Evona enlisted the help of a few friends, who in turn each contacted four others and they followed the same pattern until there were a sufficient number to collect polling lists from surrounding towns and cities, names from auxiliary organizations, town and city directories, etc. When that job was finished, Evona and her committee had collected more than 3,000 names of women who were to be invited to the tea on the terrace of the Curtis Hotel in Lenox, one of the attractive resort hotels in the Berkshires.

Then the girls began the task of addressing envelopes for the engraved invitations which were sent to the committee from the Kennedy headquarters in Boston. To make sure no one would be slighted, the invitation was reproduced in an advertisement in *The Berkshire Eagle's* social page, making it clear all women were welcome, regardless of party affiliation.

On the afternoon of the tea there was a bright sun, the sky was blue and a comfortable breeze swept across the terrace of the hotel.

More than 2,000 women turned out for the event.

Writing in *The Berkshire Eagle*, A. A. Michelson, the political reporter for *The Berkshire Eagle*, wrote:

"At one of the most effective political come-ons ever promoted in the Berkshires, 2,000 women were attracted Saturday to the gardens of the Curtis Hotel to sip tea, shake hands and gossip with Mrs. Joseph P. Kennedy, wife of the Boston millionaire and former Ambassador to the Court of St. James, and with her son, Congressman John Fitzgerald Kennedy, Democratic candidate for U.S. Senator."

"In sheer numbers," Michelson observed, "it was the greatest women's political rally ever staged in the area since women were given the voting franchise more than 30 years ago. In every sense, the party was a success.

"The Kennedys, who footed the bill, were satisfied; the women, most of whom were bedecked in Sunday's finest, enjoyed themselves; and several milliners and dress shop operators of the county, who were in attendance, were more than satisfied because it was responsible for an unusual end-of-the-summer run on hats, frocks, and shoes.

Michelson referred to Jack's play for the women's vote by quoting this from his speech:

"For some strange reason there are more women than men in Massachusetts and they live longer. Secondly, my grandfather, the late John F. Fitzgerald, ran for U.S. senator 36 years ago against my opponent's grandfather, Henry Cabot Lodge, and he lost by only about 30,000 votes in an election where women were not allowed to vote. I hope by impressing the feminine electorate that I can more than take up that slack."

The candidate's mother, who the night before was strolling along the Champs-Élysées in Paris, spoke briefly. Mrs. Kennedy flew from Paris to New York and then in a chartered plane to the Pittsfield Airport to attend the tea.

When Jack finished speaking, a receiving line was formed with the candidate standing between his mother and his sister, Patricia, who drove from Boston to attend the party. For more than an hour they greeted each of the 2,000 women in attendance, plus a number of men and children who came onto the lawn from the sidewalks where they viewed the festivities.

As we entered the hotel to pick up our belongings, Jack invited a few of us to his suite. When he sat down to rest after standing for such a long time, his sister, Pat, walked over to him, kissed him on the cheek, saying:

"Hey Kid, you were terrific!"

Jack smiled broadly, talked with his mother a moment and looked around for Frank Morrissey. It was September 7, 1952.

"Let's call Dad," said Jack, asking his mother and sister to stand by.

When the call was completed to Hyannisport, Frank handed the telephone to Jack.

"Happy birthday, Dad. Everything went beautifully up here. Great party."

Then Mrs. Kennedy and Pat talked with the former ambassador, offering birthday greetings and describing the tea. In a short time, the family broke up and went in separate directions — Jack, Frank Morrissey, and Bob Morey in a car, headed toward the next county of Hampden, bound for Springfield; Mrs. Kennedy and Pat to the Pittsfield Airport where they boarded a chartered plane to return them to Cape Cod.

13

1952
Capeless Enters the Race

Pittsfield's youthful Mayor Capeless's ambitions to seek a higher office in the state after meeting Jack Kennedy came as no surprise to friends close to him. When Jack kept repeating in his speeches across the state that young men should enter the political arena, Bob Capeless, a popular politician on the home front, got the message and plunged into a four-man race for the Democratic nomination for attorney general for the commonwealth.

Bob's technique of campaigning was new to Massachusetts. He was not wealthy. He had a good record as the city's chief executive. He was not too well known outside of the western part of the state. He could not afford elaborate political headquarters across the state. Neither could he spend too much for travel to generate support of his candidacy. He hit on a unique idea which garnered for him much publicity as he started a tour of the 14 counties in the state. He rented a house trailer, which served as his living quarters, office and campaign headquarters, paid for from meager contributions to his committee.

One of his law partners, Abraham Chesney, served as his

campaign manager and sometime driver of the house trailer. Abe was a sincere, dedicated man whose job was to persuade people who failed to share full-fledged enthusiasm for Capeless, as he did, especially Congressman Kennedy, who had a battle of his own to contend with in trying to unseat Henry Cabot Lodge.

Time and time again, Abe persisted in asking me to have Congressman Kennedy endorse Bob Capeless for the Democratic nomination for attorney general. Bob tried, unsuccessfully as did I, to explain to Abe that Jack Kennedy could not be partial to any candidate in a primary contest. Abe wouldn't buy it and before Bob and I realized it, Abe, on his own, issued a statement to *The Berkshire Eagle* that he would not support Kennedy for the U.S. Senate, but would work actively for Henry Cabot Lodge. The story was given prominence on a split page in *The Eagle*, without Abe's picture, but the "great announcement" seemed to have little effect on the readers. Many laughed, as I did, but it was embarrassing to Bob and in a way to myself.

Abe did not know that when I was asked to locate a Kennedy-for-Senator headquarters in the Hotel Wendell, that John Ford, treasurer of the Kennedy campaign, informed me the congressman would not need it until after the primaries and that Jack wanted Bob Capeless to use the space as his headquarters in his bid for the nomination for attorney general. The agreement was that if both won, they would share the headquarters through the election, with the Kennedy committee paying the bill for the entire period. Neither did Abe know that during a visit to Boston, I kept an appointment at the state headquarters for Jack with Capeless.

At any rate, Capeless placed second in the four-man race and thereafter became Jack's campaign manager in Pittsfield and in the Berkshires for the senatorial campaign.

After Jack had defeated Lodge, there was a movement in Pittsfield to hold a testimonial dinner for Mayor Capeless. I informed Jack of the plans and inquired about whether he would be able to attend, explaining that Abe Chesey was one of the leaders of the movement.

In a handwritten letter, Jack replied:

"I would of course come, Chesney or not, if they held a testimonial for Bob if I was invited — so you perhaps could let me know on this."

In my letter, after the primaries, I suggested that the hotel quarters I had rented appeared to be too small for the action I had expected to follow, and I suggested he give me permission to expand the area in the hotel.

"As to taking over the hotel," he wrote, "I think that it would be better to wait until '56 or '57 — and then report on a future trip, and on what I have been doing in Washington.

"Meanwhile I would be glad to come up for a speaking engagement — although I don't think it would be good to come anyplace where tickets were being sold. I will leave the matter to your judgement."

14

September 12, 1953
Wedding at Newport

A few days after Evona and I received an invitation to attend Senator Kennedy's wedding to Jacqueline Bouvier at Newport, Rhode Island, I received another invitation to attend a stag party for the senator at the Parker House in Boston.

The party was made up of close friends of Jack's, all young amateurs in politics, many of whom I had previously met on the campaign trail.

On the day of the wedding, Evona and I were vacationing on the Connecticut shore, not far from Newport. We decided to leave the day before the wedding and spend the night at a hotel overlooking Narragansett Bay.

At the reception, we took our places in line with hundreds of other guests. As we approached the newly married couple, Jack beamed when he shook hands with Evona.

"How about a little kiss, Evona?" said Jack as he introduced us to Jacqueline. "Have a good time," he added, "this is a great day."

15

1955
Books for New Mothers

After his wedding in Newport, Rhode Island, in 1953, Jack continued to keep in touch with key people throughout the state, but his personal visits to cities and towns were curtailed because of his back ailment, and subsequent operation.

However, members of his staff in both offices, Boston and Washington, either telephoned or wrote letters to keep his close associates up to date on his condition and personal service he was continuing to render to his constituents.

As an example, his administrative assistant, Ted Reardon, started a project on the senator's behalf which kept the Kennedy name in front of the public.

In the fall of 1955, Ted wrote to me explaining that "Jack is allotted 10 books a month, entitled *Infant Care*, published by the Children's Bureau of the Department of Health, Education and Welfare, and is most desirous of getting as much use out of them as he can."

My job was to "find a way to send us twenty-five names of new mothers each month from the Pittsfield area."

The task was not difficult since *The Eagle* carried daily a list of births from the city's three hospitals with names and addresses of the new parents. These were sent almost daily to Ted Reardon in Washington. He in turn forwarded to Jack any notes I had included with the birth announcements, as Ted put it, "in order that Jack can be kept informed on things in your area."

16

May 1956
Jack Plays Marbles and Jump Rope

After he had recuperated sufficiently from his operation, Jack was ready to return as soon as possible to the area he had not covered since being elected to the U.S. Senate and asked me to fix up a schedule.

He was in demand more than ever when I made it known he was planning a visit to the Berkshires. Frank Morrissey and I finally worked out a two-day schedule which included a tour of federal flood control projects in the northern part of the county as well as South Berkshires, and three communion breakfasts the following Sunday morning.

He tied in his Berkshire visit with an appearance he scheduled the night before in Amherst, where he spoke on "The Issues of 1956," at a session sponsored by the Western Massachusetts Citizenship Clearing House, made up of four area colleges, Smith, Amherst, Mount Holyoke, and the University of Massachusetts.

I worked out the details of his visit to North Adams and Adams with County Commissioner James A. Bowes, a former mayor of North Adams, and in South Berkshire with Michael Sullivan, chairman of the Board of Selectmen of Lee, a retired state police sergeant.

After his speech in Amherst, Jack decided to spend the night there at the Lord Jeffrey Inn, near the Amherst College campus. We agreed to meet the next morning halfway between Amherst and North Adams, so I could ride with him to the Berkshires and fill him in on developments in the area since his last visit.

Upon arriving at City Hall in North Adams, he was greeted by state, county and city officials as well as representatives of the Army Corps of Engineers in charge of the multimillion-dollar federal flood control project.

After the North Adams inspection was over with, the party of officials went to nearby Adams to look over another flood control project. There were about 20 in the group. All walked through the narrow streets through the textile mill area and Hoosic River. When they arrived at the site of a new dam the engineers were eager to show Jack — Jack was missing.

I retraced our steps since starting out toward the river and located him in an alleyway on his knees playing marbles with five youngsters, not one older than eight. He saw another group of children skipping rope on the sidewalk and then he got right into the swing of things, holding one end of a rope with a little gal at the other end, turning it until all had a chance to skip.

The children loved it. To think a man would play with them — all were too young to know he was a senator, and when he sat down on the stoop of one of the houses to chat with the group he told them who he was, and said:

"I'm Jack Kennedy, when you go home tell your fathers and mothers you met Senator Kennedy today."

As usual, Morrissey had his pad and pencil going, getting

the names of the children, their addresses, and parents' names. In a few days they received letters telling of the visit, and signed by Senator JFK.

Beaming with delight, the children ran off in various directions as Jack smiled and caught up with the group of officials who were waiting for him on the riverbanks to inspect the federal flood control work going on in Adams.

The senator's secretary, Frank Morrissey, and chauffeur, Bob Morey, left us in Adams to go to Southern Berkshire where we agreed to meet in Lee at the District Court room to discuss flood control problems along the Housatonic River.

The senator expressed a desire to stop along the way for lunch and he invited two or three others to join us. We stopped at a popular restaurant, The Springs, in New Ashford, where Jack was filled in by a few of the natives on the town's reputation for being the first to report its presidential election returns during the 1920s.

17

1956
Robert Kennedy in Charge

The candidate's brother, Bob (Robert F. Kennedy), headed the Kennedy for Senator campaign committee, keeping in constant contact with the "secretaries" scattered around the state.

A few weeks after Jack had announced his candidacy, thousands of copies of a newspaper promoting Jack for the Senate seat arrived at my home for distribution to secretaries in towns and cities in the Berkshires. A short time later I was authorized by the treasurer of the John F. Kennedy for United States Senator Committee to establish a Kennedy headquarters in Pittsfield, solely for the use of Kennedy workers and not to be tied up with the Democratic City Committee or candidates seeking other elective offices.

On one whirlwind trip of the Berkshires, Jack was scheduled to give two speeches one evening in Pittsfield. He was always late for his engagements, but the crowds seemed to wait for his arrival, regardless of the time. Instead of driving to the Berkshires by automobile, Jack decided to fly in a chartered plane to the Pittsfield Airport with the estimated time of arrival at 8:15 p.m. Lighting at the airport left much to be desired and some concern was expressed that an effort be made to have as many friends as possible in the area, drive their own vehicles to the airport.

On that particular night at least 20 volunteer supporters drove to the airport to cooperate in the plan to light up the landing field. The plane came in without mishap and Jack went on to his speaking engagements, arriving two hours late at each, but the enthusiastic supporters had remained at the halls, demonstrating no concern over his tardiness.

The following day, Jack visited the north gate of the General Electric Company to shake hands with the workers as they started their day at the plant. In the afternoon, he met with leaders of the labor union at GE and before leaving expressed a desire to visit the Black minister of the city's only Black church, the Rev. Dr. Nevers, a highly respected clergyman in the city.

As the campaign drew to a close, I had hoped Jack would receive the endorsement from my newspaper, *The Eagle*, for the seat in the Senate, but two days before the election, the newspaper endorsed Lodge. When the first edition came out, I telephoned Jack's headquarters in Boston, read him the editorial and waited for his reaction. There was none at the moment, and then, sensing my disappointment too, he asserted:

"Don't let it bother you, John. We are going to win anyway."

When the votes were counted in Berkshire County, Lodge carried the 30 towns and two cities over Kennedy, but when the returns were completed in Suffolk County in the eastern part of the state, Jack piled up a majority of over 125,000 votes over the incumbent and won the election by nearly 70,000 votes.

18

1956
"Have You Got Any Money?"

After the flood control session in Lee, we returned to Pittsfield, and then went to the hotel where Jack telephoned his wife in Hyannisport to fill her in on the Berkshire trip. That evening Evona and I decided to invite the senator to be our guest at dinner at the Country Club of Pittsfield. And he agreed it would be a great way to spend a relaxing evening after a busy day and a 7 o'clock a.m. Mass and communion breakfast — the first thing on his schedule the following morning.

At dinner, many of the guests at the club came to our table to be introduced and chat with the senator. It thrilled me because I remembered the majority of this Country Club group did not support him four years before when he opposed Henry Cabot Lodge.

The next morning he arose at 5:30, then met me in the hotel lobby at 6 for the 12-mile trip to Lee for the Berkshire Hills Council, Knights of Columba Mass and communion breakfast. A large group of parishioners and members of the K. of C. were on hand outside the church when we arrived at 6:55.

When the grand knight informed the senator that the front

row was reserved for him, he tugged on the sleeve of my coat, asking me to join him.

When Mass began, he whispered:

"Do you have a Rosary or missal?"

I handed him my Rosary. That was the last I ever saw of the beads.

When the collection was about to be made, he whispered again: "Have you got any money?"

I handed him two $1 bills, which he dropped into the basket.

Attendance at the communion breakfast, which was scheduled for the Parish Hall of St. Mary's Church, was so large that the K. of C. officers shifted it to the Morgan House, the town's best restaurant.

This was to be his major address in the Berkshires, although arrangements had been made for him to attend two others that morning.

Radio Station WBEC in Pittsfield, owned by the Miller brothers, publishers of *The Berkshire Eagle*, had approached me about taping his address for broadcast later in the day. I had not informed Jack of this move on my part until we were seated at the head table.

He mildly objected to the broadcast arrangement I had made, but then consented if I would promise to listen to the tape and correct any errors before it went over the air. Little did I realize then that my over-eagerness to get him as wide exposure as I could on his visit would develop into a near political catastrophe which developed later.

When the breakfast ended in Lee, we headed north to Pittsfield to keep an engagement to speak at the communion breakfast of the Pittsfield Police Department at St. Joseph's High School auditorium. From there we went to the Hotel Wendell where 500 women were attending the annual communion breakfast of the Rosary Society of St Mary's Church.

Monsignor Marshall, the pastor of St. Mary's, was at the door to meet Kennedy when he entered the ballroom. He escorted the senator to the head table while the women gave him a standing ovation. After he spoke, he remained in the ballroom to shake hands with every woman in the place. Even waitresses got in line to greet the senator.

The next stop on the schedule was at the newsroom of *The Berkshire Eagle*, where on Sunday mornings it was customary for the editor, Pete Miller and a few newsmen to check on the out-of-town Sunday newspapers and their mail. I had mentioned to Pete and A. A. Michelson, *The Eagle's* political reporter, that if time permitted, I would drop by the office with the senator for a visit.

Jack was concerned about the radio tape he had made at the Lee breakfast earlier in the day and asked me to be sure and check it before it was aired. Fortunately the radio station's studio was in the same building, above the newsroom. I left Jack to visit with Pete and Michelson, while I went to the studio to listen to the tape. It took about 30 minutes to hear the tape, then erase a few portions which seemed unclear. When I returned to the newsroom, Jack, Pete, and Abe gave evidence of having had a pleasant conversation and we left for the hotel where his car was waiting to take him to the Albany (New York) Airport for a flight back to Washington.

19

1956
A Political Bombshell

After the senator left for Washington, I returned to *The Eagle* to start writing my stories for Monday's edition, satisfied that the two-day tour was a success.

What I didn't know until after reporting for work Monday morning was that Abe Michelson also had a Kennedy story, the result of the meeting he and Pete Miller had with the senator while I was in the radio studio listening to the tape of the K. of C. address.

Abe normally covered the appearances of politician's tours of the Berkshires, but so long as I was with Jack on this one, I covered his county speeches.

But did Abe have a better story?

The Democratic State Committee held the headlines in newspapers across the state at the time. As he did in 1952, Senator Kennedy was supporting Adlai Stevenson for the Democratic nomination for President. A movement was on within the state committee to make Congressman John McCormack — a favorite son candidate from Massachusetts — the Speaker of the House of Representatives. To the Kennedy supporters, it appeared to be a move to help Governor Averell

Harriman of New York block the Stevenson drive.

William H. Burke of Hadley, an onion grower and tavern owner, who was the Curley-type politician in the state, was chairman.

Although he did not speak publicly about his desire to rid the state committee of machine politicians, in private conversations with his friends, he was anxious to see some new faces on the committee, men and women who would command respect from the party followers. He was determined to bring the Democratic State Committee away from those in control at the time, especially the chairman, William "Onion" Burke.

This, I learned later, was the subject of his conversation with Pete Miller and Abe Michelson in *The Eagle* newsroom when I was absent.

With the help of Larry O'Brien of Springfield and Kenny O'Donnell of Worcester, Jack's two top coordinators since he was elected to the Senate plunged into the state committee battle, visiting uncommitted members, as well as supporters of Burke.

Abe wrote that "in an interview" at *The Eagle*, Senator Kennedy said the re-election of Burke as chairman of the Democratic State Committee would be "a serious mistake." His story was carried by the Associated Press, made headlines in the Boston papers that afternoon and the news soon reached the senator in his Washington office.

While I was sitting at my desk, looking over the afternoon edition of *The Eagle*, my telephone rang. It was Jack calling from Washington.

"What happened up there, John?" he asked angrily, "that

visit I had with Abe Michelson was not to have been an interview. I was just having a friendly conversation and now the lid is off."

I looked around the newsroom for Abe. He had left for the day.

It seemed that sparks were coming out of the phone as the senator continued his verbal lashing of the paper's political expert.

There was nothing I could say, except to explain I was not in on the conversation he had with Abe and was sorry it happened.

"Well everyone in the state knows how I feel now anyway," he said as his temper seemed to simmer down. "We'll just wait now and see what happens," he added as he hung up.

What followed was that Senator Kennedy catapulted into the leadership of the Democratic Party in Massachusetts. At the election of a new state committee chairman a few days later, Burke was ousted and in his place went the senator's candidate for chairman, John M. (Pat) Lynch, a former mayor of Somerville.

20

1956
Never Underestimate Nixon

A lthough his visits to the Berkshires became less frequent in 1955 and 1956, he kept abreast of happenings in the state through reading newspapers from every part of the commonwealth.

In June 1956 he sent me a letter taking exception to a column written by Richard V. Happel in *The Berkshire Eagle*, in which he stated that:

"I have a four-room apartment in Boston in which I almost never spend a night in the apartment, which is used mostly by the senator's staff.

"Both of these statements are in error. I have lived in this apartment for ten years, have used it continuously when I have been in Massachusetts and it has been completely satisfactory to my needs. It has never been used as an office by members of my staff.

"If you think it wise, you might illuminate Mr. Happel on this."

After he lost the vice-presidential nomination to Senator Estes Kefauver at the Democratic National Convention, I happened to be in Washington and visited the senator at his office. At lunch we discussed the convention, agreeing that despite the loss, the exposure he received made him a national figure.

I asked him whether he would be a candidate at the 1960 convention and he smiled, asserting, "but not for the second spot. If I go, I will go all the way for the top job."

The conversation switched to Vice President Nixon's strength with the voting public and he quickly commented: "Richard Nixon is one of the best politicians in the business today. He is astute, clever, and knows the game. Never underestimate him."

21

1957
Lunch at the Senate

E arly in 1957 during my trip to Washington to visit Evona's mother in Georgetown, Jack invited me to have lunch with him at the Senate dining room. I met him at the appointed hour in the Senate reception room when he came off of the floor.

He introduced me to Senator Barry Goldwater, informing me he was to join us for lunch. They discussed Senate affairs for a few minutes, obviously relating to some measure under debate in the chamber at the time. Jack, during the conversation at lunch, mentioned to Senator Goldwater that I was a Navy veteran. When he asked about my Navy days, he was pleasantly pleased to learn I had been enrolled at the Navy's Indoctrination School at the University and especially interested to discover I served aboard ship in the South Pacific with one of his close friends in Phoenix, John F. Sullivan.

A few days later I received a letter from Senator Goldwater, who wrote:

"John F. Sullivan is one of my closest friends, even though we live on opposite sides of the political fence. I served for a short time with him on the Phoenix City Council and have known him all of his life. He is one of Arizona's outstanding young men, one whom I hope will continue in politics as we need his kind. Quit thinking about Arizona and come out and visit us."

Throughout the spring and summer, I kept Jack informed of activities in the Berkshires, sending him clippings on area problems that I thought would be of interest.

In the fall of 1957, with the assistance of Frank Morrissey, I helped to arrange a two-day schedule for Senator Kennedy in the Berkshires.

A non-partisan election was underway in Pittsfield at the time. When news of the senator's impending tour became known, friends of the incumbent mayor, Raymond L. Haughey, who was seeking re-election, made several attempts to have me arrange a visit by the senator to the home of the mayor, who was suffering from a virus infection.

The senator's tight schedule would not permit such a visit, neither did he want to get involved in a non-partisan election.

Ever since he was elected to the U.S. Senate in 1952, Jack, in speeches around the state, had encouraged young people to take a more active part in politics and if possible to seek elective office.

One who followed his advice was a young surgeon in Pittsfield, Dr. Jeffrey Wheelwright, the father of five children, who were friends of close friends of the senator and his wife, Jacqueline. Dr. Wheelwright had decided to enter a ward contest for the School Committee in the city. His opponent was the incumbent, Francis Douglas, a parishioner of St. Theresa's

Church, located in the heart of the ward.

Before Dr. Wheelwright entered the race, Jack had indicated to me that the next time he visited Pittsfield he would like to arrange his schedule so that he could make a social call on the Wheelwrights, whom he had not seen in some time. We found a free evening on his two-day tour and accepted the Wheelwrights' invitation to their home for a buffet and to meet a few of their friends, one of whom I was especially attempting to meet: the senator, Bruce Crane of Dalton, president of Crane & Company, a civic leader in the area, a member of the Governor's Council, a prominent Republican and son of Winthrop Murray Crane, former governor of Massachusetts and former U.S. Senator.

In addition to Mr. and Mrs. Crane, the Wheelwrights invited among others, the editor of *The Berkshire Eagle*, Laurence K. Miller and Mrs. Miller.

Jack was delighted with the evening, having an opportunity from the campaign trail to discuss with the guests an assortment of subjects. To him it was a relaxing time.

The next day *The Eagle* carried a short story that the Wheelwrights entertained the senator at their home, and supporters of the mayor became incensed. Anonymous calls poured into my home from many supporters of Mayor Haughey, charging, as one woman did, that "If you think your friend Jack Kennedy is going anyplace in politics, he'll need the Haughey people in back of him."

To make matters worse, reports were circulating in Pittsfield at the time that Dr. Wheelwright's only interest in running for a post on the School Committee was to get rid of the Catholic teachers in the school system. On top of that, Jack was informed that Dr. Wheelwright was being opposed by the pastor of St. Theresa's Church, whether for the same reason or not could not be determined.

A few days after leaving the Berkshires, Jack was on a flight to the Midwest to keep a speaking engagement. Apparently the religious overtones he heard in Pittsfield bothered him, for he wrote to me this handwritten letter on United Air Lines paper:

"Many thanks for your letter and for the help in covering my visit. As you said, I got several letters about the Wheelwright dinner. I think the priest up there should be reprimanded by the Bishop for attempting to make a religious war out of a school election. And then they complain about Al Smith's treatment."

Still disturbed over the "religious war" in Pittsfield, Jack sent me another handwritten letter a few days later. This time he wrote from Washington on U.S. Senate stationery. His short note said:

"I hope you are going to follow up on that literature handed out by that priest in Pittsfield against Wheelwright. We all complain about what happened to Al Smith and then look at what happened. I think you should take it to the Bishop who is a top-grade man."

The bishop, the Most Rev. Christopher J. Weldon of Springfield, was visiting Pittsfield at the time the second letter arrived. I showed it to him at the rectory of Sacred Heart Church where he was making an official visit. He said he would look into it, adding, "I'll be in touch with Jack."

That was the last I heard of the matter and Dr. Wheelwright was defeated in his bid for election to the School Committee.

22

1958
A Visit to Washington

J ack was out of the city when Evona, Joan, Jonathan and I were in Washington for a short visit. Jonathan was then 10 years old and at an age I thought he would enjoy a tour of the Capitol, especially a visit to Senator Kennedy's office. Upon our arrival, Ted Reardon, the senator's administrative assistant, and Evelyn Lincoln, his secretary, gave Jonathan the red carpet treatment, taking him on a guided tour of the senator's office, describing the photographs, paintings of ships on the wall, trophies, and other memorabilia. To top it off, they arranged for a private tour of the Department of Justice by an FBI agent for Jonathan, who spent two hours going through the department from the office of the director, J. Edgar Hoover, to the firing range in the basement of the building.

Being a close friend of Senator Kennedy's had some amusing sidelights in 1958 when he was seeking his second term in the U.S. Senate. One friend in the small town of Hinsdale, about 10 miles from Pittsfield, enlisted my aid through the senator's office to obtain from government surplus a Civil War cannon to be placed on the lawn of the village library as a soldier's monument. Another group wanted to cut red tape in obtaining an allotment of trout from the federal hatchery for a lake in Pittsfield. An unemployed trucker wanted to see if I could assist him in having the Department of Public Works hire his truck on a federal highway project. A Coast Guard friend was anxious to get a billet during the summer with a Coast Guard Reserve unit. And a Catholic priest sought help in saving his rectory from being torn down in an urban renewal project.

The usual visits to the area for smaller audiences diminished in 1958, because the complexion of the campaign changed in comparison with earlier years.

Larry O'Brien was in charge of coordinating all of the senator's appearances throughout the state. He called me to the Kennedy headquarters in Springfield to discuss arrangements for another trip to the Berkshires. On this trip, Larry explained, the senator would be accompanied by his wife and his brother, Ted. It was Jacqueline's first visit to the Berkshires.

Arrangements were made to hold a mammoth Kennedy "meeting" at Bousquet's Ski Lodge and then head north to make stops in Adams, North Adams, and Williamstown.

The schedule called for the Kennedys to attend Mass at St. Joseph's Church at 11, have breakfast at our home, and then leave to fill the other arrangements.

When we drove in my station wagon to the church, two Pittsfield police officers recognized the senator, his wife, and his brother, and offered a police escort to his next stop. Although the senator graciously declined the offer, he made sure I supplied him the names of the police so he could write them a letter of appreciation later.

After arriving at my house, Jack explained to Jacqueline that he visited the house in 1950 when it was under construction and recalled it was only a frame at the time. They inspected the patio and terrace, leading Jacqueline to comment:

"This is beautiful, so quiet and restful. I would love a place like this someday."

At the Bousquet Ski Area Ski Resort, about five miles from our home, a crowd of 500 showed up for the meeting. Most of them were as eager to get a glimpse of Mrs. Kennedy as they were the candidate.

When Jacqueline was called upon to speak and introduce her husband, she stepped before the microphone, hesitated a moment with an obvious shyness behind her beauty and told the crowd:

"And now, here is Ted's brother, Jack." She stole the show.

That marked Jack's last visit to the Berkshires.

After rolling up an unprecedented 900,000 vote margin over his Republican opponent, Vincent Celeste of East Boston, he concentrated his political activities the next year in campaigning across the country for the Democratic presidential nomination.

23

1960
JFK and the Words of Lincoln

J FK delighted particularly in quotations such as Lincoln's: "Public opinion is everything. With it nothing can fail, without it nothing can succeed."

His message at the centennial of the Emancipation Proclamation is at the Lincoln Memorial; and he liked to quote Lincoln: "There are few things wholly evil or wholly good. Almost everything, especially of government policy, is an inseparable compound of the two, so that our best judgment of the preponderance between them is continually demanded."

Demolishing the age argument brought up by Truman in a TV press conference, July 4 (1960), during the primaries, JFK said: "Mr. Truman asked me if I think I am ready. And I am reminded that 100 years ago, Abraham Lincoln — not yet President, and under fire from the veteran politicians, wrote these words: 'I see the storm coming and I know His Hand is in it. If He has a place and work for me, I believe that I am ready.'

"Today I say to you — in all humility — that if the people of this Nation select me to be their President, I believe that I am ready."

24

1960
Drew Pearson and General MacArthur

O n July 10, 1960, three days before Jack was nominated at the Democratic National Convention in Los Angeles as the Presidential standard bearer, Drew Pearson in his syndicated column quoted General Douglas MacArthur as saying "Senator Kennedy should have been court-martialed" for letting a Japanese destroyer "mow him down" in his PT–109.

I had read the column while Evona and I were vacationing with friends at Beach Park, Connecticut.

Pearson quoted the former commander in chief of the Pacific theater as saying:

"Those PT boats carried only one torpedo. They were under orders to fire it and then get out. Kennedy hung around, however, and let a Japanese destroyer mow him down. When I heard about it I talked to his superior officer. He should have been court-martialed."

When I returned to Pittsfield I found in the back issues of *The Eagle* since I had left on vacation, that a young former PT boat commander in Great Barrington, William F. Barrett, had taken exception to Pearson's column.

Barrett, a Republican, and a former member of the Board of Selectmen in Great Barrington, had been on patrol in the Solomon Islands the night Jack's PT boat was destroyed.

Incensed with Pearson's story, Barrett issued this statement to *The Berkshire Eagle*:

"For the record, PT's carried either two or four torpedoes, usually four. Furthermore, Kennedy did not hang around; he had fired his torpedoes when his boat was cut in two during the course of the engagement. Further, our group of torpedo boats was operating under Admiral Halsey, commanding forces in the South Pacific and not, to the best of my knowledge, under General MacArthur, who was in command of the Southwest Pacific theater then. If the general had really wanted to have Jack court-martialed, he would have had to go through Halsey and, believe me, that would have been the neatest trick of the war."

Recalling events that took place the night Kennedy's boat was cut down by the Japanese destroyer, Barrett continued:

"We were stationed across Blackett Strait and the approach to Kolombangara and Hunda in the Solomon Islands. It was obvious to the enemy we were there. Soon after arriving on station, their (Japanese) planes began to drop flares to guide their surface craft and we were subjected to steady strafing and bombings ... "

Barrett explained his was one of the few PT boats equipped with radar. He said without radar, one couldn't see a thing except when shells exploded and gave light. He added that he had not heard about Kennedy's boat until the next morning when he went to the Russell Islands to reload torpedoes in his craft.

Barrett quoted Admiral Samuel Eliot Morison's history, *Breaking the Bismarcks Barrier*, in which he described how Kennedy's boat was slit by an enemy destroyer. Kennedy helped save one member of his crew as he "clinched between his teeth the tie of the life jacket of his badly burned engineer and towed him."

Barrett added that "Jack was later awarded the Navy and Marine Corps Medal for heroism in this action, an award which we all felt did not do justice to the actual deed. However, the high brass never did pay much heed to the upstart PT service, and many acts of heroism went entirely unrewarded."

When I finished reading Barrett's statement in *The Eagle*, I sent the clipping to Senator Kennedy at his office in Washington.

The next day he sent a reply, thanking me for the clipping, adding "I was wondering if you could write MacArthur and send him this article and find out whether he ever made this statement."

That night I sent the clipping and a letter to General MacArthur at the Waldorf Astoria Towers, asking whether he ever made the statements, and reminded him that I went ashore with him at Leyte when he made his famous return to the Philippines

Two days passed and a special delivery letter came to *The Eagle* newsroom for me from General MacArthur in which he said that he gave no interview, he had never met Mr. Pearson, and the quotation attributed to him (General MacArthur) was false.

The Complete Letter from General Douglas MacArthur

90 CHURCH STREET, ROOM 1303
NEW YORK 7, NEW YORK   1 September 1960

Dear Mr. Mahanna:

I have your letter of August 30th with its enclosed clipping. The quotation attributed to me is false and does not reflect my views. I regard Senator Kennedy's service in the Pacific War as that of a brave and resourceful young naval officer. His decorations were well earned.

I gave no interview to the author of the article you mention and, in fact, have never personally met him. He attempts to put words in my mouth which I have never uttered. I can sympathize with Mr. Barrett, but at the same time would advise him not to believe everything he sees in print.

Your paper is incorrect in saying that I was a candidate for President in 1952. On the contrary, I was an ardent and loyal supporter of Senator Taft and his views and still am. At his personal request I was the Keynote Speaker at the Republican Convention in 1952.

Your letter recalled very vividly days that now seem long, long ago. The world has turned over many, many times since then. It is always a pleasure to hear from my former comrades-in-arms. With best wishes,

Most sincerely,

[signature] Douglas MacArthur

Fortunately the general's letter arrived before the deadline for the afternoon editions. Over my byline *The Eagle* carried MacArthur's statement on Page One and both the Associated Press and United Press International carried it on the wire services.

It had wide coverage, appearing in newspapers from coast to coast. When it was published in the newspapers in the Southwest where Jack was campaigning at the time, he telephoned me at The Eagle office to thank me for writing to the general, adding the story broke at a good time for him and that it was having a great impact on audiences he was addressing in the Southwest.

[For the complete news article, see Appendix B, page 155.]

25

November 1960
"I Might Get Knocked Off"

Following the Thanksgiving recess in November 1960 I drove our daughter, Joan, back to Washington, D.C., where she was a student at Georgetown Visitation Junior College.

Joan, a day student, lived with her grandmother, Mrs. Edward A. Kennedy and her aunt, Eunice Kennedy, at 3407 Dent Place, N.W., a short distance from President-elect Kennedy's home on N Street in Georgetown.

One morning while spending a few days with Evona's family, I decided to take a walk down 34th Street, but when I reached N Street there were barricades at the intersection. TV cameras were set on platforms. Photographers and news reporters were standing on the sidewalk near the Kennedy home, obviously waiting for the President-elect to come out the front door.

Across the street from his home, ropes were strung around a row of trees to keep the public back from the road. I decided to join the ranks of the curious, walked across the street under the watchful eyes of police and took up a position leaning against a tree.

Suddenly the President-elect appeared on the doorstep with a stranger to me at his side. TV cameramen focused on the pair, photographers started shooting pictures and reporters began bombarding them with questions.

In a few minutes I learned the "stranger" was Governor Sanford of North Carolina, who had been invited to the Kennedy home for a conference. After the governor departed in his limousine, Jack stepped back to the doorway of his home, waving to the onlookers across the street.

Glancing down the line of people, he noticed me leaning against a tree. He took the microphone at the public address system on the steps of his home, and then pointing to me, said:

"Hey, John, what are you doing over there?"

With that he sent a secret service man to bring me across the street. As we shook hands and exchanged a few words, the newspapermen crowded around us to listen to every word.

He was curious to know how I happened to be in the neighborhood and expressed disappointment he did not know I was to be in Washington at the time.

"I would like to talk with you longer, John," he said, looking at his watch, "but I have to get to the hospital in a few minutes to see Jackie and the baby."

"Could you stop by tomorrow morning?" he asked, "I do want to talk with you."

He beckoned to his secret service man to check his schedule the following day.

"How about dropping by at 10?" he inquired, "and we'll have time to have coffee and talk for a while before I go up to the hospital."

"Fine," I replied. "I will be here at 10."

With that he went into his house and as I looked around for a taxi to take me downtown, the reporters quizzed me about our relationship — what we talked about and why he invited me to return the next day.

Briefly, I explained we had been friends since World War II and later in Massachusetts when he entered politics. Just then a taxi came by. I hailed it and was happy to get away from the excitement and experience I had not expected to happen.

The following day my sister-in-law, Eunice Kennedy, drove me from her home on Dent Place to the Kennedy home on nearby N Street. The same group of newsmen were there, together with Stephen Rosenfeld of *The Washington Post* whom I hired originally as a reporter back in Pittsfield on *The Eagle's* county staff.

The secret service man guarding the door had my name on his clipboard appointment sheet, and admitted me inside the house.

Once inside, I was informed by Jack's butler that "the President will see you in just a few minutes. Make yourself comfortable in the living room."

After being escorted to the living room, I sat down and could hear shrieks of laughter in another part of the house. Jack and his daughter Caroline were playing hide-and-seek. He was enjoying the game as much as Caroline. Soon the door opened and the President and Caroline entered. Both shook hands and Caroline, dressed in a snow suit, explained she was about to go for a walk with her governess. With that she kissed her father, graciously shook hands with me again and went outdoors.

The President and I discussed briefly the election campaign, his happiness over being the proud father of a son, and then he became engrossed in the tremendous job ahead, forming a cabinet, getting people he wanted into important government positions.

"Would you be available, John, if something came up down here in government where I could use your services?" he asked.

I was stunned, thought for a minute and then realized you don't turn down an offer like that from the President of the United States.

As I slowly recovered from the shock, I explained I would like to discuss it with Evona and also my editor, Pete Miller.

"Do you think Pete would give you a leave of absence?" he asked.

He noticed I was hesitating because I had never been confronted with a problem like that before.

"Well, wait a minute," he said, as he reached for a telephone and called an aide requesting that he pave the way for me to get a Civil Service Form 57 from the Civil Service Commission. Jack gave me instructions as to where to pick up the necessary papers, then suggested that I think over what he had said, talk with Evona and my editor, and fill out the Civil Service papers anyway because he would have someone from his staff contact me soon.

The clock showed his time was approaching to leave for Georgetown Hospital to see Jackie and his son, John. "I hope you can come down," he said, as we walked toward the door.

"The reason I am anxious to have you pick up Civil Service

papers is because I want that protection for Evona and the children," he explained.

"Who knows?" he said, "I might get knocked off and you would possibly be out of a job."

Election-wise I understood his reasoning, never realizing how often later I would recall his words.

[For the complete news article, see Appendix B, page 158.]

26

March 1961
JFK's Message About Physical Fitness

For several years I had been attending the annual dinner meetings in New York of the Association of Camp Directors of Western Massachusetts. In 1961 when President Kennedy launched his physical fitness program, I saw an opportunity to bring it to the attention of this group.

After receiving an invitation to address the camp directors at the Statler Hilton, I wrote to the President suggesting that perhaps I could deliver a personal message from him on the importance of working into their summer camps schedules a plan suggested by the Chief Executive.

When the letter arrived at the White House, Ted Rearson, who was a roommate of the President's brother, Joseph P. Kennedy Jr., at Harvard, and now a special assistant to the President, telephoned me at my newspaper in Pittsfield informing me the President liked the idea and instructed me to pick up at the hotel upon my arrival, the message which would be wired to me.

At the same time, I thought additional support could be given to the program if I could obtain a statement from the noted heart specialist, Dr. Paul Dudley White in Boston, who was honorary president of the YMCA Camp Becket in the Berkshires. He too sent a message for me to deliver for him.

I withheld from the association's dinner committee the subject of my talk that evening until I took my place at the head table, seated next to Maxwell Rabb, a one-time secretary to Henry Cabot Lodge when he held the U.S. Senate seat from Massachusetts, and also served as secretary of the U.S. Cabinet under President Eisenhower.

Max and I had been friends for many years. His brother was a legislative counsel in Boston for the Western Massachusetts camp directors. When I showed Max the telegram from President Kennedy and the message from Dr. White, he requested the toastmaster to shift the lineup of speakers and put me on last. Max was scheduled that year to be the principal speaker, but he cut short his address, mentioning that I had a far more important message to deliver.

Here is the message wired by the President from the White House:

"I am happy to extend greetings to the Western Massachusetts Association of Camp Directors and my best wishes for the continued success of the contribution its members are making to strengthen the fitness of American youth.

"We do not want in the United States a nation of spectators. We want a nation of participants in the vigorous life. This is not a matter which can be settled from Washington. The real responsibility starts with each individual family. It is my hope that American parents will be concerned about this phase of their children's development, that the communities will be concerned to make it possible for young boys and girls to participate actively in the physical life and that men and women who have reached the age of maturity will concern themselves with maintaining their own participation in this phase of national life."

Dr. White, in the message I delivered for him, pointed out that "Despite our commendable zeal in the well-being of our young children and teenagers, we have been very remiss in neglecting in large measure the health of the most critical years of life of our young men in the 15 years between the ages of 18 and 33.

"During those years much of the good that we have accomplished at earlier ages is dissipated and the commendable habits of positive health measures are abandoned on the pleas of pressure of work, of social engagements, of financial stress, of lack of time, or of just plain carelessness ... Those involved in the education of the young, physically and spiritually, as well as mentally, have a responsibility to extend their service to the all-important twenty- to thirty-year-olders.

"We are planning a pioneer program for this third decade of life at Camp Becket next September, and hope that others may accept this challenge in the not-too-distant future. This may be a turning point in our crusade against most of the diseases still so common in the U.S.A. today."

The reaction to both messages was enthusiastic as many camp directors volunteered they were going to write to the President to assure him they would support his fitness program at their summer camps.

I hurriedly left the hotel to find a Western Union where I

could file a story for *The Eagle* in Pittsfield. I couldn't write an advance on the speech I was to deliver because I did not have the material until I arrived in New York only minutes before the dinner meeting began.

[For the complete news article, see Appendix B, page 160.]

27

1961
Interviewing for a Job
with the Federal Government

Less than a year after President Kennedy moved into the White House, one of his procurement aides explained in a letter to me that I might be interested in coming to Washington to be interviewed for a possible appointment in the federal government.

My Civil Service papers had been filed a few months before and I learned through friends in Pittsfield that they had been interviewed by investigators for the Civil Service Commission about my background and experience as a reporter and editor.

When I arrived at the Executive Office Building next to the White House, for a conference with one of the President's staff members, I learned that a number of appointments had been set up for me with various government officials in such places as the U.S. Information Agency, the Federal Aviation Agency, the Department of Commerce, the State Department, the Peace Corps, and others.

At each of the offices I visited over a three-day period, secretaries would usher me through to the offices of high officials, all appointees of President Kennedy, one of whom best described my visit with each by asserting, "You come here with pretty strong credentials, the President himself." I could sense they had been alerted that President Kennedy was eager to get me placed in his administration.

I recall my interview at the Peace Corps because I did not seem to have the qualifications to serve with that group, which was headed at the time by President Kennedy's brother-in-law, Sargent Shriver.

After that interview, Richard A. Graham, director of recruitment for the Peace Corps wrote to me, explaining how much he enjoyed our meeting, and added:

"I am afraid that I could have saved you some time had I read your Form 57 a little more carefully when you came in.

"You have an excellent background and I am sure you could be of great help to us in public information or in public affairs. However, a further examination of your biographical data indicates that you were at one time a special agent with the Office of Naval Intelligence.

"I believe you can understand the reasons for a policy which renders ineligible anyone who has had an intelligence background. Many of the nations who have requested Peace Corps volunteers are particularly sensitive to charges by other nations and by their own people that the Peace Corps may have intelligence overtones. We want to make it absolutely clear that this is in no way true."

The last stop on my appointment list was the Pentagon. Arriving early for the appointment with the director of public information for the Office of Civil Defense, I decided to use the free time by calling on Ralph (Rip) Horton, a close friend of President Kennedy's since the days they were classmates at Princeton before the President transferred to Harvard.

Rip at the time was serving on the staff of the Secretary of the Army. We discussed the appointment arranged for me with the Office of Civil Defense, an agency I knew little about.

My interview with the public information director of Civil Defense, C. Owen Smith, was so short that I was at first left with the impression he was only going through the motions in seeing me and reporting to his superior that I had kept the appointment.

In less than five minutes, after he hurriedly read my Form 57, he walked from behind his desk and said: "You are just the man we are looking for. You'll be hearing from us soon." With that he left and went across the hall to the office of the Assistant Secretary of Defense for Civil Defense, Steuart L. Pittman, for whom I later served as a staff assistant.

A short time after I returned to my job as county editor of *The Eagle*, I received a telegram informing me of my appointment as a public information officer with the Office of Civil Defense at the Pentagon in Washington.

Days went by before I made formal acceptance of the appointment. I discussed it with my wife, my publisher, fellow editors, reporters, relatives, and friends. It was a hard decision to make because my security was with *The Eagle*, where I had been employed for several years, but at the same time I wanted to be a part of the Kennedy team in Washington.

During the days I was trying to make a decision, Evona and I were invited one Sunday afternoon, following the Boston

Symphony Orchestra's concert at Tanglewood in Lenox, to a reception at the home of Mrs. Olga Koussevitzky, widow of the famed conductor of the Boston Symphony, Dr. Serge Koussevitzky. His successor as conductor, Charles Munch, was among the guests. We became close friends after he joined the BSO, playing golf and attending social functions during the summer months.

While Evona and I were talking with Dr. Munch in a corner of the terrace of Mrs. Koussevitzky's estate, I mentioned to him the opportunity I had to join the Kennedy administration in Washington and showed him the telegram offering me the post.

In his best English, the French conductor looked at me and said:

"You must go. This is the President talking. In France that would be an order."

A few days later I notified the Office of Civil Defense that I would accept the appointment, but not until I gave my employers, the Miller brothers, time to find a successor.

28

October 1962
The Cuba Crisis and My Debut
Working for the Office of Civil Defense

My report date at the Pentagon was October 15, 1962. The bus route from Georgetown in Washington — where I was staying temporarily with Evona's mother and sister, Eunice — to the Pentagon presented a problem because I was not familiar with the system of transferring from a District of Columbia bus to one going to the Pentagon in Virginia.

I managed to locate a bus going near the State Department near Constitution Ave and 23d Street where I was instructed to board a Virginia bus which stopped at the Pentagon.

While I waited near the State Department for a bus going to the Pentagon, I could see overhead helicopters whirling by. Some were flying toward the White House, while others going in the opposite direction, I discovered later, were landing at the heliport at the Pentagon. It was an eerie feeling. I didn't know what it all meant.

When I arrived at the Pentagon there seemed to be an air of tension in the concourse and corridors as I walked toward my new office. It was the kind of a silence I had not experienced since my days in the Navy just before an amphibious operation.

After reporting to the public information office of Civil Defense, I was assigned to a desk, loaded with an assortment of periodicals on fallout, shelters, radiological monitoring, medical self-help, atomic bombs, instructions to homeowners in case of a nuclear attack, etc.

The apathy I had toward Civil Defense as a newspaperman soon disappeared as I read more and more about the national program which began to make sense to me. For the first time, I started to realize why President Kennedy wanted me in the Civil Defense agency.

When I read the text of his message to Congress on Civil Defense, May 25, 1961, I was convinced he had placed me in an important position. In his message to Congress, President Kennedy said:

"One major element of the national security program which this nation has never squarely faced up to is civil defense. This problem arises not from present trends but from national inaction in which most of us have participated. In the past decade we have intermittently considered a variety of programs, but we have never adopted a consistent policy. Public considerations have been largely characterized by apathy, indifference, skepticism; while at the same time, many of the civil defense plans have been so far-reaching and unrealistic that they have not gained essential support.

"This administration has been looking hard at exactly what civil defense can and cannot do ... the history of this planet, and particularly the history of the 20th century, is sufficient to remind us of the possibilities of an irrational attack, a miscalculation, an accidental war, or a war of escalation in which the stakes by each side gradually increase to the point of maximum danger which cannot be either foreseen or deterred. It is on this basis that civil defense can be readily justifiable — as insurance for the civilian population in case of an enemy miscalculation. It is insurance we trust will never be needed, but insurance which we could never forgive ourselves for foregoing in the event of catastrophe."

That was the day President Kennedy signed an executive order, assigning responsibility for the civil defense program "to the top civilian authority already responsible for continental defense, the Secretary of Defense," Robert S. McNamara.

Little did I realize that while reading his message to Congress, President Kennedy was at his desk in the White House meeting with the National Security Council, the joint chiefs of staff from the Pentagon, his cabinet and staff, faced with the discovery in Cuba of Soviet missiles aimed at the United States.

Not until October 22, 1962, a week after I had reported for work at the Pentagon, did I realize that we were on the brink of war, threatened by a nuclear attack from Cuba. When President Kennedy went on nationwide television that night to speak on the crisis of Cuba, only then did I fully understand the responsibilities of his office of President, and the responsibility he had assigned to me.

29

1963
Correcting Mistakes in a Book

S eptember 9, 1963
Dear Mr. President:

I am enclosing a copy of a letter I have written to Victor Lasky, calling to his attention errors in a paragraph concerning me which appears in his new book, *J.F.K. — The Man & The Myth.*

I have also sent a copy of the letter to the Macmillan Publishing Company and to your father in Hyannisport.

Sincerely,

John G. W. Mahanna, Staff Assistant

Enclosure

*

September 5, 1963

Mr. Victor Lasky

c/o The Macmillan Company New York, New York

940 25th Street, N.W.

The Potomac House Washington, D. C.

Dear Mr. Lasky:

I have just read your book entitled *J.F.K. — The Man & The Myth — A Critical Portrait.* I was very amazed to read your remarks on Page 88 which concern me and which remarks are very far from the truth.

The paragraph which concerns me reads as follows:

John Mahanna, of *The Berkshire Evening News,* a newsman covering the U.N. Meeting, later commented that Kennedy had one thing going for him as a reporter that very few of his colleagues had — entree. "On the strength of his father's contacts," he said admiringly, "Jack could call top officials, United States and foreign, from the hotel lobby and go right up for interviews."

I wish to state:

1.   I have never worked for *The Berkshire Evening News.* In fact, there is no such newspaper. I did work for many years for *The Berkshire Evening Eagle* in Pittsfield, Massachusetts.

2.   I have never covered a United Nations meeting, either as a reporter for *The Berkshire Evening Eagle* or for any other news media. I was in San Francisco in April 1945 as an officer with the Office of Naval Intelligence, 12th Naval Intelligence Headquarters, spending my full time in the Service.

3.   I have never made statements regarding President Kennedy and his father, such as you attribute to me on Page 88, nor have I ever made remarks of a similar nature to anyone.

Your reference to me, and the quotations which you attribute to me, have caused me considerable embarrassment. I ask that you immediately make a retraction of this entire paragraph. In the event your book should be published in future editions, I request that the paragraph concerning me be deleted.

Your remarks quickly call to mind the words of Mark Twain: "Someone is handling the truth mighty carelessly around here."

I shall hold you, and the publisher of your book, responsible for all damages that may be sustained by me, or by members of my family, as a result of your publication of these untruthful remarks.

I might call to your attention footnote 3 on Page 84, wherein you conclude "However, the former Pacific Commander-in-Chief promptly denied having made any such statement." It would have been the truth if you had continued on to say that General Douglas MacArthur when questioned about the court-martial incident by John G. W. Mahanna of *The Berkshire Evening Eagle*, Pittsfield, Massachusetts, gave Mr. Mahanna an exclusive report promptly denying having made such a statement. General MacArthur stated to Mr. Mahanna that he never talked with or met Drew Pearson, and he had never made the statement to Drew Pearson or to anyone else.

Very truly yours,

John G. W. Mahanna

JGWM: map

September 9, 1963

Dear Mr. Kennedy:

Enclosed is a copy of a letter I have sent to Victor Lasky, author of the book, *J.F.K. — The Man & The Myth*, which contains a paragraph erroneously quoting me. I have also sent a copy of the letter to the President.

I hope this letter finds your health improving every day. My job with the Assistant Secretary of Defense for Civil Defense is interesting. The President's new Civil Defense program is getting off the ground with a favorable report from the Armed Services Committee. Now we are about to watch developments on the floor of the House.

Evona joins me in sending to you best regards.

Sincerely,

John G. W. Mahanna, Staff Assistant

Enclosure

Mr. Joseph P. Kennedy   Hyannisport, Massachusetts

J.Mahanna/cn

*

September 9, 1963

Dear Larry:

Enclosed is a copy of a letter I have sent to Victor Lasky and the Macmillan Publishing Company relative to the errors in his new book, *J.F.K. — The Man & The Myth*, in a paragraph attributed to me. I also have sent copies to the President and Mr. Kennedy.

Sincerely,

John G. W. Mahanna Staff Assistant

Enclosure

Mr. Lawrence F. O'Brien

Special Assistant to The President The White House

J. Mahanna/cn

(Identical letter sent to Pierre E. G. Salinger Press Secretary to the President)

30

1962 and 1963
JFK's Letters

S oon after becoming a government employee, assigned to the Defense Department in the Office of Civil Defense as a public information officer, I joined the National Press Club.

As I widened my acquaintanceship with the Washington press corps, I met Fred Blumenthal, who with Jack Anderson, were the Washington editors of *Parade* magazine.

Fred and his wife, Dorothy, were living in a townhouse in Foggy Bottom, across the street from an apartment house where I resided. During one of Fred's visits to my apartment for a buffet supper, I showed him several letters from President Kennedy that I had saved over the years.

He was intrigued with the changes in the signature from the early days of our correspondence to the time he entered the White House and asked if he could make copies of a few to send to his editors at *Parade's* New York office. Fred wanted to do a feature story on the signatures and I agreed, but not to the contents of the letters.

When the story appeared in the *Parade* supplement it was circulated across the country in Sunday newspapers.

Parade boasted a circulation of about 12 million copies at the time.

Shortly after the *Parade* article reached the homes of readers throughout the United States, I started receiving letters from people informing me of letters they too had saved with the President's signature. The majority of them missed entirely the point of the article. They were under the impression I was a collector of President Kennedy's letters and wanted either to buy them or offer them for sale at auctions.

Apparently this misunderstanding resulted from the lead of the Blumenthal story in which the writer pointed out that "A few weeks ago, a letter in the handwriting of the late John F. Kennedy — written to the widow of a PT-109 shipmate — was auctioned in New York for $9,500, and other examples of Kennedy handwriting and signatures command premium prices."

"The letters," the article explained, "are from a collection of a close personal friend of the late President, John G. W. Mahanna, former county editor of *The Berkshire Evening Eagle*, Pittsfield, Mass. The friendship between the the two men dated back to Mr. Kennedy's days as a reporter immediately after World War II. The two corresponded on personal and political subjects all through Mr. Kennedy's Congressional, Senate and White House career until the time of his death. Often the two corresponded in longhand, and even when he dictated, Mr. Kennedy sometimes tacked on handwritten postscripts. He frequently dashed these off so quickly that they were almost illegible."

Letters addressed to me by people with Kennedy signatures started pouring into the newsroom of *The Berkshire Eagle* in

Pittsfield because the *Parade* article gave no indication of any other address. Similar letters were beginning to arrive at the *Parade* magazine office in New York. It was an impossible task to attempt to answer them and finally *Parade* prepared a form letter, explaining the misunderstanding, and these were mailed after more than 1,000 letters had been received.

Here are a few of the examples of letters received:

If this letter is of any value, I am sure it would help me in my old age and arthritis.
Greeley, Colorado

Enclosing a photostatic copy of a Kennedy letter for your pleasure. The original I would like to dispose of to the highest bidder?
St. Petersburg, Florida

(This one was addressed President John G. W. Mahanna)
I have a personal letter from President Kennedy that I will sell. I also have a bronze medallion from the official inaugural. There were only 4000 of them made. I would appreciate any help.
Largo, Florida

Mrs. _____ has a personally autographed picture as described in Parade. We would welcome your opinion as to whether or not this item has a value as a collector's item.
New York City, N.Y.

I'm sending you a copy of a original sig of our Dear late President John F. Kennedy. Is there any value or market for this ...

I read in the paper that one of his letters was worth quite a bit.

Franklin, Ohio

I wish to inform you that I have the signature of our late beloved President Kennedy ... It has been a prize to me. If you are interested please let me hear from you.

Portland, Maine

I have an autograph of the late President Kennedy..I wondered if you could advise me of what this autograph is worth or where I could sell it. I am not a collector and could certainly use the money better than the signature.

Bradenton, Florida

Read with a great deal of interest Fred Blumenthal's account of your JF Kennedy collection. Of all the President's I have known I liked and admired Kennedy the most.

Kirkwood, Tennessee

I have two letters signed by President Kennedy. Are they worth anything?

Etowah, Tennessee

In 1959 and 1960, I wrote letters to J.F. Kennedy. He answered them – in typewritten – signed by longhand – he answered three plus a Christmas card. Is is possible I could sell the letters and Xmas card : I have no bank account, and, due to social security, I'd be "willing" to sell them. Yet there are wonderful memories of a wonderful person.

St. Petersburg, Florida

I had a glossy photograph from Mr. Kennedy in which he had wished me best of health, autographed it for me ... Things are kind of rough and I thought if I could possibly get any kind of amount of money from this it would sure help.

Silver Spring, N.Y.

I have a set of pictures in technicolor that were made by my husband during the 1960 campaign when President Kennedy made a speech in Roanoke, Va ... The pictures are so good that my husband took them to Mr. Sam Rayburn, a personal friend of many years, and Mr. Rayburn was so pleased with them he took my husband to show them to the President shortly after the election. The President was also enthused and thought no campaign picture had been as good. He autographed the set of eight and asked for three himself, Mr. Rayburn got one and my husband kept the other four ... Can you tell me how to go about contacting collectors who would be interested in buying the four pictures, all different poses?

Kingsport, Tennessee

I have a letter written by President Kennedy which I cherish as a personal communication from him. The signature shown on the attached true copy is in ink. I would like to request your opinion on whether it is his own.

Baton Rouge, Louisiana

As you may know, President John F. Kennedy was a magnificent human being, to the destitute and the well-to-do alike, here in West Virginia. As he sat on a decayed log, smiling and bareheaded at the mouth of a coal black mine, talking to the dirty-faced, underfed miners, his every word fell like pearls upon such desolation. His words breathed life into such downtrodden communities. We believed in him and loved him for his goodness.

Two days after his election to the office of President of the United States – I wrote him a little note, telling him how happy we West Virginians were that he had won. To my delight and surprise he answered the note himself – He typed the little note, with haste and sincerity, making at least three mistakes in his typing – Then he signed the note in a flourish, just like signature number 5 that appeared in *Parade* in our local paper. I've shown the little letter, with pride, to hundreds of friends. Its magic has brightened my life. I'm considered an important person in our little community because I received a real, honest-to-goodness letter from John F. Kennedy signed in his own handwriting.

Amma, West Virginia

When he was in Massachusetts, I had the grand opportunity to be with him ... I asked him to autograph a "Five Dollar Bill." ... Also he autographed a book of matches..and I also had a black fox muff, which I treasure dearly since he put his hands on it. Of course, you know what a wonderful sense of humor he had. If you could direct me to the right person, I may be willing to give up all three articles to an auction.

Hull, Massachusetts

Can you give me an in idea of the value of a picture I have of President Kennedy. I received it about 30 days before his assassination ... I have no intentions of selling it but for personal interest would like to know. Also I'm thinking of insuring it. And incidentally I'm 15 per cent Irish and it was my great admiration for the President that prompted my wife to enlist the Governor's help in getting it for me. It took almost a year as the Cuban crisis interfered at one time.

Yakima, Washington

Would you be interested in signature of JFK? I have one signed by him. Can you use it in an auction for his library? I know my son would like to be in his library. He gave his life for his country too. My son received the Silver Star and several mentions.

Crocker, Missouri

I understand that such signatures are increasing in value, and having such a signature wonder if you are in the market for purchasing the same ... The circumstances surrounding my signature are these. In the summer of 1958, I took my family to Washington and Congress was in session ... My daughters were interested in collecting signatures of important persons. While downstairs in the Senate we saw John Kennedy standing alone. I said to one of my daughters, "Get that man's signature and you may be getting the signature of the next President of the United States." My daughter did so and I shall always remember his gracious smile as he took a few moments asking about herself and the state of Georgia. Even though we hold a high sentimental value for the signature, my daughter, who is now in college would be willing to sell it. I would appreciate very much your noting the approximate price which such signature might be worth and let us know if you are interested in the purchase.

Decatur, Georgia

One of my more treasured possessions is a letter I received from him, typewritten, but with his signature. It seems like he still ought to be here. Mr. Mahanna, I don't think I am some nut, but it was interesting to read about your letters from this great man. I just wanted to tell you about my little one.

Silsbee, Texas

I have a letter written by him when he was campaigning for President. I was wondering if you would know where it could be auctioned or sold to someone collecting such.

Ballston Spa., N.Y.

I feel I have a rare as well as an unusual personal letter from Mr. Kennedy ... If you are interested in contacting me regarding these mementoes, I will be happy to discuss the above with you.

Dayton, Ohio

I see in today's *Globe* you are saving our friend John F. Kennedy LETTERS. I gave a few that Pres. sent me in 1952 when running for Congress and Sen. to my Grand-Children and them to save to go to college. I forgot how many letters and I

did not want to raise their HOPES of college until I found out
if worth cash – kindly let me know.

Boston, Massachusetts

I would like to inform you, that I have two letters, signed by
him, if they are of value or interest to you, kindly advise.

Danbury, Connecticut

Just after election in 1960 I received a letter from President
Kennedy. The letter and signature are in perfect shape.

Reluctantly I would like to sell it. Can you help me?

Waterloo, New York

Read in the Parade where you have letters from John F.
Kennedy and that maybe you would help me sell my letter
from him. Help me God I hate to part with it but I need the
money for Dr. and Hospital Bills.

Sioux Falls, S.D.

I just came across a letter I received from the late John F.
Kennedy. I wondered if this signature is of any value to you.

Stoneham, Massachusetts

I have at home a menu from a banquet which my husband
and I attended in 1959 in memory of our late President Grover
Cleveland. Out late President John F. Kennedy was guest of
honor and I was fortunate to shake his hand and have him
autograph my menu. The menu also has a picture of our late
President, at that time a United States Senator of

Massachusetts. If this would be worth anything to you, I would be glad to send it to you.

Buffalo, New York

I saved two letters of many. If you are interested you may have them. Any money received will go to the Morgan Memorial ... You see I knew old Joe ever since they lived at Oyster Harbor ... I know Jack would approve of my donation to the M.M. summer camp for poor kids.

West Newton, Massachusetts

Can you contact Mr. J.G.W. MaHanna, ex-editor? I have three political letters John F. Kennedy wrote me and I will sell them. Way below what the one sold in New York, $9,500. Please be do kind as to contact him so we can talk this over.

Evansville, Indiana

We are one of the many families that have had misfortune and always need money. I am writing to you because you may know a collector that is interested in buying an original (John Kennedy) signature: I feel that we need the money and he would want us to have it!

Valparasso, Indiana.

Would appreciate any information you might give me relative to value of JFK signatures.

Winthrop, Massachusetts

Appendix A

Timeline
of John G. W. Mahanna and JFK

1913 July 3

John G. W. Mahanna is born in Lenox, Massachusetts, the son of the late Timothy A. and Mary A. Fitzgerald Mahanna.

1917 May 29

John Fitzgerald Kennedy is born in Brookline, Massachusetts.

1929 July 28

Birth of Jacqueline Bouvier (the future Jackie Kennedy) in Southampton, New York.

1929 October 24

Beginning of the stock market crash (ended November 13) which ushers in the Great Depression, which lasts until 1939.

1930

Mahanna graduates from Lenox High School, where he was editor of the school newspaper, and president of his senior class.

1933

Mahanna begins working at *The Berkshire Eagle* newspaper, in Massachusetts.

1933 March 4

Franklin D. Roosevelt (FDR) is sworn in as the U.S. President.

1939 September 1

World War II begins when Germany invades Poland and then, two days later, France and Great Britain declare war on Germany.

1941 October 4

John G. W. Mahanna marries Evona Kennedy of Pittsfield.

1941 December 7

Japan attacks the U.S. naval base at Pearl Harbor, on the island of Oahu, Hawaii.

1942 July 24

Mahanna is commissioned as a warrant officer in the Navy, assigned as a special agent with the Office of Naval Intelligence.

1942 to 1945

During his war service, Mahanna writes special dispatches for *The Eagle,* and on his return he covers the local reaction to the Japanese surrender.

1943

Mahanna is promoted to chief warrant boatswain and recommended as lieutenant junior grade. He is sent to the University of Arizona for indoctrination before being assigned to amphibious forces in the South Pacific aboard the USS Heywood.

1944

During World War II, Mahanna and Kennedy meet briefly when both are serving in the navy in the South Pacific.

1944 June 6

D-Day: Allied forces launch a surprise air, land and sea attack on Nazi-occupied France.

1944 June 15

Mahanna participates in D-Day assaults with the Marines on nine islands in the South Pacific, serving as a communications secretary.

1944 August 12

Joseph Patrick Kennedy Jr. (born on July 25, 1915), the older brother of JFK, is killed in action. Posthumously, he will be awarded the Navy Cross.

1944 November 7

Franklin D. Roosevelt is reelected for a 4th term as U.S. President.

1945 April

Mahanna accidentally meets Kennedy at the UNCIO Conference in San Francisco, and they quickly become friends.

1945 April 12

FDR dies in office, succeeded by V.P. Harry S. Truman.

1945 July 24

Mahanna is honorably discharged from the U.S. Navy. In addition to the Presidential Unit Citation, he receives nine battle stars as well as the Liberation Medal for the Philippine campaign.

1945 August 6 and August 9

The U.S. bombs two Japanese cities, Hiroshima (August 6) and Nagasaki (August 9).

1945 September 2

Japan surrenders, ending World War II.

1947 September

John G. W. Mahanna is appointed county editor of *The Berkshire Eagle*.

1948

Mahanna introduces "Congressman Kennedy" to the Berkshires, and arranges a series of appearances for Kennedy.

1952

When Congressman Kennedy runs for the U.S. Senate, Mr. Mahanna's wife, Evona, is chairman of a tea at the Curtis Hotel in Lenox in Mr. Kennedy's honor. It is the first big tea party of a series throughout the state to promote the Kennedy candidacy.

1953 September 12

Senator John F. Kennedy and Jackie Bouvier are married in Newport, Rhode Island.

1954

Mahanna prepares an informative and historical booklet for the 45th annual golf tournament of the state association.

1954 October 21

JFK undergoes a spinal operation, is near death, and requires long months of recuperation. This was the second of the four spinal surgeries Kennedy underwent between 1944 and 1957.

1955

Mahanna's news story "Hawthorne's 'Little Red House' at Lenox is being restored" is published as a brochure.

1955

Mahanna is commissioned to write a history of the Berkshire Symphonic Festival, *Music Under the Moon: A History of the Berkshire Symphonic Festival, Inc.* The ebook is downloadable from Hathi Trust Digital Library: https://www.hathitrust.org.

1956 January 1

JFK's book *Profiles in Courage* is published, comprising short biographies of eight courageous American senators during pivotal moments in American history. The book becomes a bestseller, and wins a 1957 Pulitzer Prize.

1956

JFK misses the Vice Presidential nomination, but becomes a nationally known figure.

1957 November 27

Birth of Caroline Bouvier Kennedy, daughter of Jacqueline Kennedy and Senator John F. Kennedy.

1957 to 1959

Campaigning for the presidency, JFK criss-crosses the USA.

1960 November 8–9

JFK is elected as the 35th U.S. President. The election was held on November 8, with 303 electoral votes for Kennedy versus 219 for his Republican opponent Richard M. Nixon, who conceded on November 9.

1960 November 25

Birth of John F. Kennedy, Jr., son of Jacqueline Kennedy and President-elect John F. Kennedy.

1961 January 20

Inauguration of John F. Kennedy as the 35th U.S. President.

1961 March 20

Mahanna delivers, to members of the Association of Camp Directors of Western Massachusetts, messages on physical fitness from President Kennedy and Dr. Paul Dudley White.

1962 October 5

At the request of JFK, John G. W. Mahanna (age 49) leaves his job (as county editor) at *The Berkshire Eagle* newspaper, to take a job as public information officer with the U.S. Office of Civil Defense. His office is in the Pentagon.

1963 November 22

President Kennedy assassinated in Dallas, Texas.

1984 December 10

Death of John G. W. Mahanna.

1994 May 19

Death of Jackie Kennedy Onassis in New York City at age 64.

1999 July 16

John F. Kennedy Jr., son of Jacqueline Kennedy and President John F. Kennedy, dies in a plane crash at age 38.

154   John G. W. Mahanna

Appendix B

Articles About JFK

From Chapter 24
(The complete article written by John G. W. Mahanna.)

Didn't Hit Kennedy War Record,
Gen. MacArthur Tells *The Eagle*
By JOHN G. W. MAHANNA
The Berkshire Eagle, Pittsfield, Massachusetts

(Mr. Mahanna, county editor of *The Eagle*, was a chief warrant officer in the U.S. Navy during World War II, participated with amphibious forces in several invasions in the South Pacific and the Leyte operation, when he went ashore with Gen. MacArthur on his return to the Philippines Oct. 20, 1944.)

Gen. Douglas MacArthur today branded as "false," a statement attributed to him in July by a well-known columnist that U.S. Sen. John F. Kennedy should have been court-martialed for his actions in the South Pacific when his PT boat was cut in half by a Japanese destroyer.

Drew Pearson quoted Gen. MacArthur on July 10 as saying, "Those PT boats carried only one torpedo. They were under orders to fire it and then get out. Kennedy hung around however, and let a Japanese destroyer mow him down. When I heard about it I talked to his superior officer. He should have been court-martialed."

MacArthur's Reply

Following publication of Pearson's column and a subsequent story from Great Barrington on July 21, in which William F. Barrett Jr., a PT boat commander with Sen. Kennedy's group in the South Pacific, took exception to the columnist's printed remarks. I wrote to Gen. MacArthur to clarify the issue.

This is his reply, received at *The Eagle* today:

Sept. 6, 1960
Gen. Douglas MacArthur

The quotation attributed to me is false and does not reflect my views. I regard Senator Kennedy's service in the Pacific War as that of a brave and resourceful young naval officer. His decorations were well earned.

I gave no interview to the author of the article you mention and, in fact, have never personally met him. He attempts to put words in my mouth which I have never uttered. I can sympathize with Mr. Barrett, but at the same time would advise him not to believe everything he sees in print.

(Barrett, a Republican, is a former member of the Board of Selectmen of Great Barrington.)

After Pearson's remarks were quoted in newspapers

throughout the country, Barrett came to the Democratic presidential candidate's defense. He pointed out that PT's carried either two or four torpedoes, usually four. Furthermore the Great Barrington veteran said Kennedy did not "hang around"; he had already fired his torpedoes when his boat was cut in half during the engagement.

The Eagle article at the time reported that Gen. MacArthur, former commander in chief of the Pacific Theater during World War II, was a presidential candidate in 1952. The general was widely considered a candidate prior to the 1952 Republican convention in Chicago, but never formally announced himself as such.

Supported Taft

On this point the General commented in his letter:

"Your paper is incorrect in saying that I was a candidate for President in 1952. On the contrary, I was an ardent and loyal supporter of Senator Taft and his views and still am. At his personal request I was the keynote speaker at the Republican convention in 1952.

"Your letter recalled very vividly days that now seem long, long ago. The world had turned over many, many times since then. It is always a pleasure to hear from my former comrades-in-arms."

From Chapter 25
(The complete article written by John G. W. Mahanna)

Eagle's County Editor Chats With Kennedy Over Coffee
Special to _The Eagle_

WASHINGTON — John G. W. Mahanna, county editor of _The Berkshire Eagle_, Pittsfield, Mass., and a World War II Navy friend of President-elect John F. Kennedy, was a caller at Kennedy's Georgetown home yesterday.

Mahanna was standing across the street from the Kennedy home with newsmen Tuesday when he was spotted by the President-elect and invited to make a social call yesterday morning.

The Massachusetts editor accompanied his daughter, Miss Joan K. Mahanna, here Sunday on her return to Georgetown Visitation Junior College following the Thanksgiving recess. He had been visiting his mother-in-law, Miss Eunice Kennedy, who lives only a couple of blocks from the John F. Kennedy home.

Yesterday morning he saw a crowd gathered outside the Kennedy home and stopped to see what was going on. He was leaning against a tree when Kennedy, coming out of the house with Rep. Chester Bowles (D–Conn) and Gov. Luther Hodges of North Carolina, saw him, waved and yelled, "What are you doing there, John?" He sent a Secret Service man over to escort Mahanna across the street. Kennedy told Mahanna he was on the way to the hospital to visit his wife but would like to have him drop in the next morning for a social call.

Mahanna spent 15 to 20 minutes with Kennedy over coffee

yesterday morning. He didn't disclose to newsmen the nature of their conversation but was chuckling when he came out. Asked why, he said that when he arrived he found the President-elect playing hide-and-seek with his three-year-old daughter Caroline.

Among the newsmen who talked with Mahanna was Stephen S. Rosenfeld of *The Washington Post*, son of Mr. and Mrs. Jay C. Rosenfeld of Pittsfield. Rosenfeld formerly was on *The Eagle's* staff covering the Great Barrington area under county editor Mahanna.

From Chapter 26
(The complete article written by John G. W. Mahanna)

Physical Fitness Stressed
Kennedy, Dr. Paul D. White Send Pleas to Camp Directors
March 21, 1961
Special to *The Eagle*

NEW YORK — President John F. Kennedy and Dr. Paul Dudley White last night called upon camp directors of Berkshire County to offer their assistance in helping to strengthen the physical fitness of young people in the United States.

Their measures, stressing the importance of developing a nationwide program of health among today's youth, were delivered here last night by John G. W. Mahanna, county editor of *The Berkshire Eagle* in Pittsfield, Mass., at the 15th annual dinner meeting of the Association of Camp Directors of Western Massachusetts at the Hotel Statler Hilton.

Ray Golden, director of the Camps Wahconah and Potomac in Pittsfield, president of the association, presided.

President's Message

In his message to the camp directors, President Kennedy said:

"I am happy to extend greetings to the Western Massachusetts Association of Camp Directors and my best wishes for the continued success of the contribution its members are making to strengthen the fitness of American youth.

"We do not want in the United States a nation of spectators. We want a nation of participants in the vigorous life.

"This is not a matter which can be settled in Washington. The real responsibility starts with each individual family.

"It is my hope that American parents will be concerned about this phase of their children's development, that the communities will be concerned to make it be possible for young boys and girls to participate actively in the physical life and that men and women who have reached the age of maturity will concern themselves with maintaining their own participation in this phase of national life."

Dr. White's Appeal

Dr. White, the famed heart specialist, who is honorary president of Camp Becket and who treated President Eisenhower during his illness, explained in his message the contribution Berkshire County camp directors can make in offering support to the President's Council on Youth Fitness.

Dr. White, who is planning a novel experiment at Camp Becket from Sept. 17–30 for married couples, described his message to the camp directors as "one of the most important for the health and welfare of this country that I have ever delivered."

Said Dr. White:

"Despite our commendable zeal in the well-being of our young children and teenagers we have been very remiss in neglecting a large measure the health of the most critical years of our young men in the 15 years between the ages of 18 and

35. During those years much of the good that we have accomplished at earlier ages is dissipated and the commendable habits of positive health measures are abandoned on the plea of the pressure of work, of social engagements, of financial stress, of lack of time, or of just plain carelessness."

Pediatricians Concerned

"Even our pediatricians are beginning to think that they must take a new look at their current practice during the last generation of developing over-nourished and under-exercised youngsters from infancy on without a follow-up as to the results of this program in middle age. Those involved in the education of the young, physically and spiritually, as well as mentally, have a responsibility to extend their service to the all-important 20- to 30-year-olders.

"We are planning a pioneer program for this third decade of life, at Camp Becket next September and hope that others may accept this challenge in the not far-distant future. This may be a turning point in our crusade against most of the diseases still so common in the U.S.A. today."

About 150 attended the dinner meeting held in the Ivy Room of the Statler Hilton, including several businessmen from Pittsfield and area camp towns of the Berkshires. Paul Winter, director of Camp Glenmore in Monterey, was chairman of arrangements.

Conte Sends Message

U.S. Rep. Silvio O. Conte, who was unable to attend because of committee hearings in Washington yesterday, wired a message to the meeting. In it he called to the attention of the camp directors their "duty" to aid conservation programs. He said, "We must work to preserve to make sure that we hand down to future generations the priceless heritage of our natural assets which have been ours to enjoy."

Maxwell Rabb, former secretary of the U.S. Cabinet under President Eisenhower and former confidential secretary to Henry Cabot Lodge when he served in the U.S. Senate, was among the speakers last night. Others included Daniel England, president of the City Council of Pittsfield; Lawrence J. Flynn, director of promotion for the Massachusetts Department of Commerce; John F. Downing, executive director of the Berkshire Hills Conference, and Maxwell M. Alexander, national director of the United States Association of Private Camps.

Appendix C

A Letter From John To Evona

Seadler Bay
Manus Is.
Admiralty Islands
November 1944

My Darling Evona:

It's plenty difficult these days to find something interesting to write to you and Joan. Not very much uncensorable material is left for me to mention. The days are all alike, especially the 24 we have seen go by since our return to this base from the invasion of the Philippines. It's hot. The humidity is high and the weatherman never fails to give us our daily rain.

Over on the beach Seabees continue to build this newly acquired island into a mighty base. Ships of all types come and go. Pilots practice dive bombing; larger planes roam through the sky from morning until night. Signal lights of all descriptions send a variety of messages throughout the harbor. Occasionally the presence of unidentified planes in the area sends us to general quarters but usually we wind up with a flash white which means the pilots have identified themselves as being friendly.

This afternoon I tried to think of something different to do to help pass the time out here while waiting for news of our next assignment. Finally, I decided a nice long letter to you, giving a chronological summary of the war as I have seen it, would be in order. It would be something we could read over together, get a lot of enjoyment from its contents, and could also take up an evening sometime and review it when I return to you and Joan and don civilian clothes again. Because of the nature of such an ambitious job, I will not be able to mail this letter to you right now because of censorship regulations but it will be filed with your letters in my desk until an appropriate time arrives to break it out for you to read.

Thirty-seven months ago today we were married at St. Joseph's. The weather was beautiful with the Berkshire foliage in full bloom. You were (and are) so beautiful in that adorable ivory satin wedding dress. I can see you approaching the altar, glancing to the right to make sure of my timing. For a newspaperman with a reputation for being completely relaxed most of the time, I was as nervous as a fawn on thin ice. Will you ever forget how jittery I was in trying to ease the ring on your finger? The reception which followed at your home, so attractively decorated with the autumn leaves I faithfully promised to gather, but failed to produce. Our automobile trip to the Waldorf will live with us forever. Too bad we haven't a couple of prints in our album of the accidents we met up with en route to New York.

The problems we met in attempting to redecorate our first apartment were enough to discourage any young couple but we managed to wind up with a very attractive home, thanks to you, your taste and selections of furnishings to blend with our gorgeous wedding gifts. We had fun entertaining friends except on nights when my work would take me away from you at the most inopportune times. Remember how the police would always call at dinnertime to inform me of a murder, a fire or some other bit of news in the area? It wasn't so bad when you could come along with me to cover the assignment, but it was tough on both of us when we had guests for the evening. That's life though, I guess.

We hardly ever talked about the war. Sooner or later I would be in the service. We seemed to maintain silence on that point as long as we could. Upon our return from a few days' vacation in New York, sort of a second wedding trip, we found in the mail basket at midnight just one piece of mail, a simple form card from the draft board calling me up for a screen test in the near future. Little did we realize then that a friend had already mentioned me as a candidate for Naval intelligence work. That next morning, outside the courthouse, when Lieutenant Horgan asked me whether I would be interested in making application for a job with ONI, I couldn't believe my ears. The interview which followed in the first naval district headquarters at Boston seems like a dream. Commander Mitchell, in making out my papers to take a physical examination, needed only know the name of the college I attended to complete the form. I noticed the recommendation he inserted before my name was "ensign!" A big lump settled in my throat when I saw his expression change after informing him that I didn't go to college.

"Well, how about a warrant then?" he asked, as I tried to

recover from the first blow. Knowing very little about the various ranks in the Navy at that time, I naturally inquired for further details of this specialist's rank.

"In the work you'll be doing," explained the commander, "it won't make much difference whether you are a warrant or an ensign. The pay is the same. You'll be in plain clothes practically all of the time and if everything goes well, you may stand a chance of getting a commission."

That bit of encouragement was all I needed. From that day on I vowed I would one day win for you a commission in the US Navy. The rest of the day was spent signing literally millions of papers for this, that and everything. My wrist was sore from writing my name so many times on all kinds of forms. Ordinarily it takes about three or four weeks for papers to clear through Washington but action was slow in coming on my application. Tracers were sent to the Navy department but proved unproductive.

Dental work was urgently needed in order to complete my physical. A limited time was given to have this work attended to and while our little vacation at the cottage we rented at Lake Mahkeenac didn't seem exactly like a vacation because of my dental appointments, we did have fun in our own way, bicycling (partly to take off weight) to the beaver pond which we used to visit in an effort to make some good action pictures; fishing, taking along a few sandwiches and a couple of bottles of beer; swimming, sunbathing, having guests down to listen to the records Eunice let us take for a few days; getting to church on bicycles; trying out all of the bunks in the place, including the two in the loft.

Then the day Commander Mitchell called, anxiously wanting to expedite my appointment. A few more days remained to complete the dental work and then without too much warning another call was received from Naval headquarters while I was covering the current sitting of Superior Court. Pete Miller's call to Tom gave us a few more days together and then the Eagle party and the presentation of some useful gifts from the newspaper and associates on the staff. I can remember that night as though it were only last night — the serious tone attached to it. This party wasn't like the others we had had in the past. A cloud of gloom seemed to settle over the room at Timmy Ryan's place because, I guess, no one knew how long it would be before I would be back to you for good and back to the staff too. I assure you, darling, that night has been fresh in my mind for months and months.

The following morning as I boarded the train for Boston with as much luggage as an admiral going to a new assignment, my heart was breaking because I didn't want to leave you, and I kept telling myself you were braver than I as I kissed you goodbye on the station platform. You knew I was going to return to Western Massachusetts but for some reason or other I couldn't make myself believe it would be true, and then, after reporting, I was back to you that night! The order taking me to Springfield still seemed like a dream. Tom Moriarty was the first acquaintance I met as I arrived in Springfield. Breakfast with him did more for me at the moment than anything I can recall. Inexperience in a new field, I thought, would mean weeks of study and hard work, but the assignments seemed to be of a type familiar to me in gathering information — only this time it was classified as secret, confidential or restricted.

Our little telephone chats are a wonderful memory and the commanding officer, Al Raiche, was more than fair in distributing cases so I could be with you more and more in the Berkshires. Some of those cases are nasty, others very interesting but it was difficult trying to overcome a complex I developed in fighting the battle of Western Massachusetts in plain clothes. I think the case I did in Vermont — just when I wanted to be with you because of the expected arrival of our little Joan — turned out O.K. I worried more about you then than at any time I can remember.

Being home with you and the family on Thanksgiving day in 1942 was a happy day for all of us. I can see you now, knowing full well that the expected was about to happen but keeping it to yourself so as not to, what you thought "spoil" the day for everyone. I was so proud of you holding out until dinner was completed and acting like a little soldier. In spite of the pain and discomfort you were suffering, you managed to smile and joke a little about going to the hospital. I was as nervous as a kitten on the keys, believe me, and during the preparation I confess, Evona darling, I don't know what kept me from breaking all the rules in the book and rushing to your side. I tried not to show my nervousness but it would have taken more than a Murat to hold me down. I think Doctor got as much of a kick out of my actions as anything that ever happened to me during all of the year I was with the Kennedy family. His instructions to me about telephoning as soon as you were taken to the delivery room are as fresh in my mind as events during the battle of Leyte only a few days ago. No time was lost in telephoning, you can be sure, and Doctor's arrival gave me the strength I needed at the moment. Soon everything was over with and Joan made her appearance in the arms of a nurse. My knees began to wobble as I saw this beautiful little girl gazing through big blue eyes at me. I couldn't believe it to be true because I guess the assurance Dr. Desautels had given to me minutes before that you were all right hadn't sunk in. I didn't believe it until I saw for myself and then the picture of Joan reflected in my mind and I knew everything was just as Dr. Desautels said. I was so happy and the next morning when I came to see you again I could see too that you were as happy as I. Gee, darling, I can see you now telling me that you were "a bad girl" and me giving you assurance that you were a "good girl" and that I loved you very much. I couldn't wait for you to see Joan and neither could I wait for some nice flowers to arrive for you. The terrible room you had made me feel badly but it didn't bother me too much because I was so relieved to know you were all right. Then when your room did change, everything turned out beautifully and flowers and cards started to pour in to you. I had to return to Springfield and each time I telephoned you I could tell how happy you were and I always loved to hear you speak of Joan's progress. Then the trip back home with Frank Scott taking charge of the "Little Charm" and the three of us in the Packard. I shall never forget how strange everything seemed to me in the baby's room after Joan returned with us. I wasn't used to seeing babies bathed, fed, changed, etc., but tried to pretend I was taking it all in stride. The beautiful basinette (is that right?) and bathinette were quite the contrivances to me. Actually I was afraid to touch Joan because she looked so fragile. As I look back on it now, I can't help but think of what a wonderful baby she was, when you hear the stories a lot of other people have to tell about their babies.

Then that awful day in June when I left you in the morning to go to the office in Springfield, write up my reports and return in the evening. I couldn't quite believe it when I walked into the office and the boys told me about my orders to Pacific Beach, San Diego, Calif., and then indoctrination school in Arizona. It was hard to telephone you the news but I had to do it and to this day I don't remember driving home. It was terrible but I tried to act calm. One redeeming feature of the whole thing was the school. I had always wanted to go to a school of this kind and I guess the time I spent there aided me later on, and best of all I knew you wanted to go to a school too. I had never traveled any great distance before. Except to Florida. But the trip went rather quickly after I got out of Chicago and met on the train some nice people, including the friend of Cupie Colt's with whom we played bridge. The boy I traveled with, Benaker, was a most uninteresting person. I wrote to you every chance I got on the trip and got great fun out of posting letters and cards of various places en route to you and the family. When I arrived in Los Angeles to transfer to San Diego, it all seemed like a dream. What was I doing that far away from you? I looked over Los Angeles from the attractive depot and wished you were with me to see the beauty of California. San Diego gave me a different picture though. Here was nothing but Scollay Square, Boston. Nothing but sailors all over the place and a crummy little railroad station. The trip from there to the anti-aircraft school about 9 miles away seemed like a hundred mile trip. I was glad to find some of the other Massachusetts boys at the school when I arrived. For some unknown reason I was the last of the group to arrive. They put us up in horrible huts for the night, then the next morning told us we could find a more decent place to live if we wished. We did just that and I was fortunate to meet a nice fellow like Larry Kennelly to room with. At night when we weren't at school we would go to the bar and watch the crowd in what they called the "Little Club" in the Grant Hotel, sort of a night club but only a nickelodeon for music. Then after 7 days we headed to Tucson. What an aggregation! A bunch of phoney boatswains who had never been to sea, minus ribbons and salty expressions, off to a school where we thought surely they will make us at least ensigns before sending us to sea. We arrived at the school a sheepish bunch, some of us scared of the academic course because it had been so long since we were in school. When we first looked at the courses we thought "we'll never make it" but a little bearing down seemed to work. As I look back now we did pretty well academically, and the military work with calisthenics thrown in did me as much good as anything I can remember. I was stiff and sore and grumbled at times but it all turned out O.K. What a thrill we used to get after classes to return to our bunks on the big gymnasium and receive our mail. Your letters inspired me more than anything I ever had happen to me sweetie but golly when I received my orders to the Heywood I didn't know what to do. I thought surely after school I would get some leave like everyone else but just the phoney boatswains got orders to "proceed." It was lucky for us that one of the boys knew a few angles and suggested a telegram to the bureau for a delay in reporting. Some didn't take the chance, like Melvin and Bob White, but Larry, Jim and I did. We knew how expensive it would be but then sweetie we were all upset, thinking we were going to sea in a strange unequipped way and probably would not see you again until the war was over.

And then I thought, if anything should happen to me, "I must see Evona and we must have a good time. I want her to be happy and remember the days we had together before leaving." I repeated this to myself, and "Nothing, not even the Navy will keep me from her or Joan even if it means a court martial." As it turned out though darling it was wonderful — all except our trip home in a lower! Ha, Ha. I shall always remember it. Quite an experience and a lot of fun, wasn't it sweetie? The return trip west after spending three wonderful days with you in Chicago and some more at home with you and Joan and Dr. and Mrs. Kennedy and the girls gave me new vigor or something. I just knew after that the thought of going to sea wasn't too bad and besides as long as I was in the Navy you were proud to see me go overseas and no one could point at me for being shore based. I will never understand why I was sent to Seattle. When you and I were at the Reamer House in Chicago, the Heywood had just left San Francisco for New Zealand. This I found out later. Then the trip down to San Francisco and no quarters. Here I was in a big city, left like hundreds of other officers to get accommodations for myself and report in to headquarters every 24 hours for transportation overseas. I thought it would be a couple of days but these turned into weeks and all we ever heard each morning at 10 at the Port Director's office was "sorry, nothing today, report back tomorrow at the same time." What was there for us to do? If they would only put us to work it would help to pass the time. The only good times I ever had there were spent with George Canrinus and his wife. They are about the nicest people I have met in the West. I became depressed all the time, worried about everything and was all mixed up financially and got to the point where I prayed to be sent overseas to get away from the routine as long as I couldn't be with you. I used to go to the hotel bar all alone in the afternoon and drink beer. It's a good thing they didn't serve liquor until 5 o'clock because I was getting beside myself and I saw all the movies and became very unhappy watching people dance and be gay. The break came when we were sent to Treasure Island toward the end of our stay to go to work loading troops. That was fun and gave us something to do. Finally the day arrived for us to go overseas and I thought "Golly, I may not see Evona or Joan for years." I felt as strange as a cow at a horse show when I went aboard that mammoth carrier to be transported overseas with hundreds of officers and enlisted men. We tried to act like veterans but somehow or other we felt conspicuous. The trip was O.K. for a while and then when a storm came up I became frightened and sea sick one day. What a feeling. The only consolation I got was writing to you and I can see myself now on the flight deck with my stationery trying to keep within censorship regulations (something new to us) and trying to write so you wouldn't worry. When Diamond Head came into sight about a week later it looked like a movie on a screen and excitement ran up and down my spine as we entered Pearl Harbor and started down the channel. It was all new and again I wished you were with me.

Not knowing the ropes, the three of us — Jim, Larry and I — checked around for more information on Honolulu, thinking we were in the heart of it. We discovered, however, that it was a half hour's ride on a bus. We couldn't wait to see the place we had read about for so many years, so we went downtown in the first bus. We were amazed to find such a filthy city. The streets were narrow; dirty and unattractive buildings filled each side of the street. We were disappointed to say the least. After our return to the Navy hard, however, we learned we didn't go far enough through the city to the residential area and real showplace of this section of the island, Waikiki. So, losing little time, the next day we took another bus right through the heart of Honolulu and our eyes were opened to real beauty when we saw the beautiful white stucco one-story buildings in Waikiki. And then the Royal Hawaiian Hotel with its beautiful palm trees and main building of Spanish architecture caught our fancy. It was a Navy rest camp for submarine men but other branches of the Navy were welcome too, so we toured the grounds and sat beneath the palm trees in the patio drinking beer and thinking of home. We even took a swim that afternoon and repeated the performance on many succeeding days. The trip downtown was a long one and some days we preferred to stay near the Navy yard because we were anxious to wait for our mail which generally came early in the afternoon. It was always a happy day when mail arrived from you sweetie. I was lonesome and kind of up in the air with this strange new life, and really didn't get settled down until my ship arrived early in

December after making the assault landings at Tarawa in the Gilbert Islands. I recall how bloody the operation was and how terrible I felt about this kind of duty from reading all the news accounts and listening to these veterans who were taking part in the amphibious operations of the Pacific. When I reported aboard I was lost. Finally I decided the best way to get along was to be honest about everything and not attempt to bluff my way as many people do, and thank God my decision paid dividends as I went along. I was assigned a nice room and some of the fellows who are one here with me today took me in hand and patiently indoctrinated me into the Navy aboard a ship. I knew I would never make a boatswain because men with 10 and 15 years' experience who are now officers said they couldn't tackle the job either. Anyway, I figured it wasn't my choice and I would do the best I could, hoping against hope for a break and a change in rank. I was sent to a gunnery school for a day — for what I'll never understand. It was upon my return from this school that I received your radio dispatch informing me of Doctor's passing. It was the worst shock I ever received in my life and I didn't know which way to turn. All of the mean thoughts I ever had about our former Executive Officer, I take back every time I think of how consoling he was. He went to every extreme to get permission from the Captain for me to return to you because he knew how much we needed each other. He didn't succeed in his efforts but I have always been grateful to him for the attempt he made.

Going to Maui for maneuvers (something also new to me) did me more good than anything at the time because I met Junior Freels, who went to Tucson with me. It was like meeting someone from home at that time, and after being with him a couple of days I kind of looked at things in another light and looked forward to the time I would be with you and stopped or at least tried to stop thinking of the past. It did help a bit and then we set out for the Marshall Islands, a place I had never heard of until we were at sea for a few days. The men on here seemed to be a little fidgety which didn't help me much but when they explained we had more protection than ever, I kind of took in the slack. When we arrived in Kwajalein and I made my debut to war I realized how much better this duty was than some of the other branches of the military service. I knew nothing about landing boats but soon learned when I was ordered to be a boat officer in charge of taking ammunition and gasoline to the beaches on Enewetak where heavy fighting was still going on. I wasn't really scared because I didn't realize the seriousness of the duty and when it was all over and I thought about it I trembled like a leaf. Getting shot at in the dark is no fun but the night that happened in pitch darkness at about 0100 in the morning I just felt lucky that the Jap snipers didn't get our range. Snipers fired on our boat lying off shore while we were waiting for the signal to deliver the ammunition needed by the Marines, but only splashes of water resulted. Through the darkness we could hear and see tracer firing near the beach where I was supposed to land but we couldn't tell whether the Japs were doing all the firing or the Marines. The firing ceased for a while and then I was ordered into the beach, gilded by only a dim red flashlight held at the landing spot by a Marine. I had orders to evacuate a Colonel and his staff to take them to a ship in the anchorage for an important conference. I remember it as well as though it were 10 minutes ago. I said my prayers, told God how much I loved you and asked to be spared and said to the coxswain "O.K. let's go." The trip was slow but sure. We made the landing O.K. but the firing started again as soon as our boat hit the beach. As I climbed from the ramp a Marine on the beach yelled "get horizontal buddy or you'll be sorry." While I don't know how long it took me to hit the beach, I'll bet it was less than 2 seconds and when the word was given "all clear" I found myself buried in the sand, having unknowingly dug a nice little fox hole. The Marine explained a Jap sniper broke loose and was firing in all directions. Some Marines killed him 25 yards away with machine guns. While waiting for the colonel and his staff, I wondered more than once "what the hell am I doing here?" Soon his party arrived and we were off to the ship. It was the grandest feeling I have ever experienced. I was in the boats again two days later at the next island on Enewetak but it wasn't very bad since I was sent into the beach in the daytime and had little trouble. I hoped and prayed I would never have to be in the boats again. My prayers were answered because that was the last time I was ordered to that type of duty. The skipper later explained he wanted me to be familiar with all phases of this work. Needless to say I acquired too much knowledge in a short space of time. Brought aboard ship during these two operations were soldiers and Marines with the kind of wounds I had read about but had never seen. Arms were off, legs dangled from their bodies, heads were split open and a few walked with bandages around their heads, arms or legs. It was a pitiful sight. I had to get used to it if I was to continue on this kind of duty and before long, like a few other officers, found myself assisting the medical department, undressing the wounded, helping to bathe their wounds and lighting their cigarettes, bringing them water and doing other little things to occupy their minds while they awaited their turn on the operating table. The work of the Navy medical department was something I'll never forget. A few hopeless cases died but many others which I thought were beyond hope survived. None of these fellows cried, became hysterical or upset. They just patiently waited for their turn and hoped for the best. It was here that I saw plasma at work. On one boy I saw the doctors supply him with four bottles of plasma and two bottles of whole blood all at once! He lived. Well, when we returned to Pearl Harbor we naturally all went ashore at the first opportunity to try to forget the terrible sights we had seen. Believe me honey, it isn't like something that happens to you in civilian life and you use it as an excuse to take a few more drinks than you ordinarily would, but our first day ashore didn't seem to be an excuse to get tight. We were so tense that everyone just unfolded and went to town. Some of the boys got tighter than others. I was among the former but afterward we all seemed to return to normalcy because of the good news from the authorities that we would go home for an overhaul. The trip was like a luxury cruise and my visit to the Western Union to wire you seemed like a dream. When I telephoned you the next day and heard your wonderful voice I seemed to wake up. Sweetheart it was all I needed. I knew I'd be with you soon and tried every which way to picture what Joan would be like too. What a thrill to arrive in New York and realize I was so close to home. I'll admit my sleeping over in the hotel wasn't timed very well and I am so sorry I missed you and Joan at the station. But honey I was so tired I must have knocked myself out in bed. When I did arrive though and saw you there in the station I felt like crying because I was so happy to be back with you, Joan and Mrs. Kennedy. And being home for Easter made it doubly nice for all of us. Leaving again after many wonderful days with you was hard for both of us. When I arrived back on the West Coast I was more lonesome than before but Jack Brannen provided good company and we had a lot of fun. There was one thing I always liked about him; he was a good fellow to be with on Liberty. You know and I know how immoral a lot of people are and what some people think of men in uniform. Jack and I used to get high a lot when we went out but we kept our self-respect and faithfulness to our wives which is more than a lot of others can say. When we received our orders to sail and I called home it made me feel miserable when I learned you were out and I couldn't reach you before we left. I tried to blame myself for not letting you know I would call but there was no previous word given to us and the orders came suddenly. A miracle must have happened because our orders were delayed later and then I was able to reach you in the afternoon and we were both happy again.

I was by now feeling like a veteran, and newer ships joining the fleet all the time seemed to give me more confidence than ever. When we were ordered to make the assault landing at Saipan it didn't seem to phase us because we now had advanced bases in the Marshalls and we knew how powerful our fighting fleet really was. It had been tested and proved itself under Admiral Halsey whenever the Jap fleet dared come out to meet his challenge. While I was no longer a boat officer, I found myself in them again when the Captain ordered me ashore to write a report of the operation. It afforded me a good opportunity to get a news story too and that is why I think the story *The Eagle* used was the best I had written to date. There is nothing I could say here that wasn't in the story except that I can show you a couple of pictures taken in the town of Charon Kanoa on the day following the initial assault. We returned to Enewetak and remained there for several days awaiting new orders. It was while here that my leg started to really bother me severely for the first time. Injections in the hip seemed to be the only comfort I could get but for some reason or other I couldn't put any weight on my right foot. Commands changed here and Captain Jones came aboard, paying me a visit in one of the Officer's rooms where I was permitted to rest instead of going to Sick Bay. After 22 days on the sick list (all during the Tinian Operation which followed and which I know little about) I returned to duty with a recommendation that I be taken to the next base hospital for consultation and possible survey. I knew these doctors didn't understand the story of my condition and consequently objected to any attempt to survey me but they insisted I would probably be kept at the hospital and eventually sent to a shore job. It seemed to me to be serious at the time and that is why I tried to prepare you for whatever might happen and it was never my intention to scare you. They had me confused until the orthopedic surgeon at the hospital at Pearl said it wasn't serious and that it was probably a condition aggravated by humidity, rainy weather and standing on steel decks too long. When we went to sea again it started all over again and I couldn't understand it but then I realized how much the weather probably had to do with it all. It rained hard every day and we were in the typhoon belt. All of the veteran doctors had been transferred previously and we had a new batch. The senior medical officer was a baby specialist; the next in line a surgeon and two interns. The surgeon, Dr. Tildes, took an interest in my case and had me go to the base hospital here at Manus for another consultation with a friend of his who was in charge of the orthopedic section and I was glad he sent me. This doctor, who reminded me so much of Dr. Kennedy, because of his nice manners and understanding disposition, made a careful check with measurements of my legs and concluded that it is a condition "which we haven't a name for but a familiar one and a common one among servicemen on duty in this climate." He explained that the humidity is so high the doctors haven't found a solution to such problems and assured me not to worry because in another climate it would probably not bother me at all. He suggested a lift be placed inside my shoe to even up the slight shortage and then to exercise by walking, playing golf, volleyball, skiing or any "damn thing you want to do." He said the confinement on board ship and lack of proper exercise, together with too many starchy foods and the climate, make a condition like this uncomfortable, and not to worry. I have the utmost respect for his opinion.

Well, to get on with the war. We then went to Leyte in the Philippines. I have never seen (and never expect to see again) as many ships as the Navy sent on this operation. It wasn't bad at all for us but some of the units caught hell after we left the area as you know. The story I have written will bring you pretty much up to date on the Philippine campaign.

That magazine story may never get published but it will be cherished by me forever because you gave me the inspiration to write it and someday I hope to be able to write a book on my experiences or things I have observed and dedicate it to "Evona and Joan," because you are part of me in everything I do and I love you so very much. I wish this letter were typed in the smooth darling but this mill is the best I have at the moment. I'll close now hoping this letter has brought to you a little picture of what has been going through my mind during all these months I have been away from you. I love you and miss you but we'll be home soon.

All my love and kisses,
John
John G. W. Mahanna

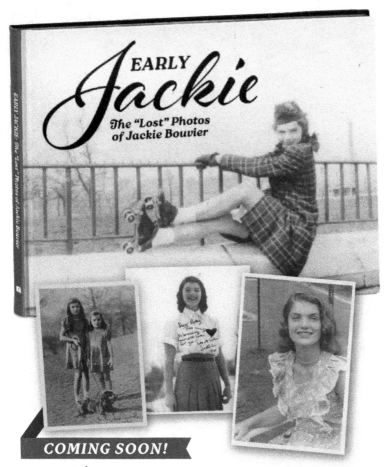

EARLY Jackie The "Lost" Photos of Jackie Bouvier

A full-color, coffee-table style photo album of 67 previously unpublished and seldom-seen photos of Jackie Kennedy from her childhood and teen years.

There must be hundreds of thousands of photos of Jackie Kennedy (1929-1994), our much-loved First Lady, either with or without President John F. Kennedy, but what you are about to experience in *Early Jackie* is strikingly different from the well-known and classic Jackie photos. These are the "lost" photos of Jackie from when she was known—prior to marriage—by the name of "Jackie Bouvier."

MAURICE BASSETT

Publisher's Catalogue

The Mahatma Gandhi Library
#1 Towards Non-Violent Politics

* * *

The Prosperous Series
#1 The Prosperous Coach: Increase Income and Impact for You and Your Clients (Steve Chandler and Rich Litvin)

#2 The Prosperous Hip Hop Producer: My Beat-Making Journey from My Grandma's Patio to a Six-Figure Business (Curtiss King)

#3 The Prosperous Hotelier (David Lund)

* * *

Devon Bandison
Fatherhood Is Leadership: Your Playbook for Success, Self-Leadership, and a Richer Life

Roy G. Biv
1921: A Celebration of Toned 1921 Peace Dollars as Numismatic Art

Dancing on Antique Toning: A Further Celebration of Numismatic Art

Dancing on Rainbows: A Celebration of Numismatic Art

Early Jackie: The "Lost" Photos of Jackie Bouvier

Sir Fairfax L. Cartwright
The Mystic Rose from the Garden of the King

Christy Harden

Guided by Your Own Stars: Connect with the Inner Voice and Discover Your Dreams

I ♥ Raw: A How-To Guide for Reconnecting to Yourself and the Earth through Plant-Based Living

Curtiss King

The Prosperous Hip Hop Producer: My Beat-Making Journey from My Grandma's Patio to a Six-Figure Business (The Prosperous Series #2)

David Lindsay

A Blade for Sale: The Adventures of Monsieur de Mailly

Rich Litvin

The Prosperous Coach: Increase Income and Impact for You and Your Clients (The Prosperous Series #1) (Steve Chandler and Rich Litvin)

David Lund

The Prosperous Hotelier (The Prosperous Series #3)

John G. W. Mahanna

The Human Touch: My Friendship and Work with President John F. Kennedy

Abraham H. Maslow

The Aims of Education (audio)

The B-language Workshop (audio)

Being Abraham Maslow (DVD)

The Eupsychian Ethic (audio)

The Farther Reaches of Human Nature (audio)

Maslow and Self-Actualization (DVD)

Maslow on Management (audiobook)

Personality and Growth: A Humanistic Psychologist in the Classroom

Psychology and Religious Awareness (audio)

The Psychology of Science: A Reconnaissance

Self-Actualization (audio)

Abraham H. Maslow (continued)

Weekend with Maslow (audio)

R. Lee Procter

The Million Dollar Sticky Note: A Story

Harold E. Robles

Albert Schweitzer: An Adventurer for Humanity

Albert Schweitzer

Reverence for Life: The Words of Albert Schweitzer

Patrick O. Smith

ACDF: The Informed Patient: My Journey Undergoing Neck Fusion Surgery

William Tillier

Abraham H. Maslow: A Comprehensive Bibliography

Personality Development through Positive Disintegration: The Work of Kazimierz Dąbrowski

Margery Williams

The Velveteen Rabbit: or How Toys Become Real

CPSIA information can be obtained
at www.ICGtesting.com
Printed in the USA
FSHW022113151021
85450FS